THE
HISTORY
OF
BREIFNE O'REILLY

The History of Breifne O'Reilly

by
Dr. J. J. O'Reilly

The Long Riders' Guild Press
www.thelongridersguild.com
ISBN No: 1-59048-105-4

To the Reader:

The editors and publishers of The Long Riders' Guild Press faced significant technical and financial difficulties in bringing this and the other titles in the Equestrian Travel Classics collection to the light of day.

Though the authors represented in this international series envisioned their stories being shared for generations to come, all too often that was not the case. Sadly, many of the books now being published by The Long Riders' Guild Press were discovered gracing the bookshelves of rare book dealers, adorned with princely prices that placed them out of financial reach of the common reader. The remainder were found lying neglected on the scrap heap of history, their once-proud stories forgotten, their once-glorious covers stained by the toil of time and a host of indifferent previous owners.

However The Long Riders' Guild Press passionately believes that this book, and its literary sisters, remain of global interest and importance. We stand committed, therefore, to bringing our readers the best copy of these classics at the most affordable price. The copy which you now hold may have small blemishes originating from the master text.

We apologize in advance for any defects of this nature.

TO MARGARET

In appreciation of her assistance
with the publication of this book.

CONTENTS

LIST OF ILLUSTRATIONS

LIST OF ABBREVIATIONS
USED IN NOTES

A.F.M.	Annals of the Four Masters.
B.A.S. Jn.	Breifne Antiquarian & Historical Society Journal.
Bealoides.	Journal of Folklore Society of Ireland.
B.N.J.	British Numismatic Journal.
C.S.P.I.	Calendar of State Papers, Ireland.
Duffy	Duffy's Hibernian Magazine.
Gen. Hist.	Genealogical History of the O'Reillys, by Prof. Carney. Dublin Institute of Advanced Studies.
I.B.L.	Irish Book Lover.
I.E.R.	Irish Ecclesiastical Record.
Kilmore.	The Diocese of Kilmore. By Philip O'Connell. M.Sc.; F.R.S.A.I.
R.I.A. Proc.	Proceedings of the Royal Irish Academy.
U.J.A.	Ulster Journal of Antiquities.

INTRODUCTION

When I set out to trace the ancestry of my family I was impressed by the amount of material which existed in relation to Breifne in general and the O'Reillys in particular. This material however was scattered throughout numerous periodicals, state documents, and scientific journals, much of it not readily accessible to the general public. It seemed worthwhile, therefore, to bring it all together in one place. While I cannot claim originality for the contents of this book, I hope that it will prove of interest and value to the numerous members of the O'Reilly family and perhaps stimulate more people to visit the present County Cavan which is sadly neglected in tourist literature despite its attractive if subdued scenery and its rich content of archaeological remains.

Much of what I have written is legend rather than history, but even legend may have value as containing a substratum of truth. Anne Terry White puts the argument for this contention very well in her book, *Myths and Legends Retold*, where she says, "A myth is an invented story, while a legend is not wholly invented—it is a kind of history; of course there may be plenty of invention and myth wrapped around a legend but always at its heart there is a kernel of historical truth." A good example of this thesis is found in Dr. Philip O'Connell's explanation of the legend of the Cailleach Geargain.

This question of legend prompts me to quote from a

remarkable article in Volume III. No. 1 of the *Journal of the Breifne Antiquarian Society* for 1927, entitled "The Coming of the UI—Briuin," by John P. Dalton M.A.; M.R.I.A. The article is in flat contradiction to the generally accepted account of the origin of the Gael.

Dr. Dalton contended that the *Leabhar Gabala (The Book of the Invasions)* "was the official charter of the Gaels, a composition having for motivation the vindication of Gaelic dominance by endowing the dominators with a indisputable seniority in the decisive qualifications of age and racial distinction. The modus operandi of its composition consisted in utilising old fragments of tradition and clothing them with a richly wrought integument of fiction."

He stigmatises the whole story of the Milesian invasion as pure legend; Mil, Eremon, and Tuathal Teachtmar were, he said, the figments of bardic history; "far from the lordly Gaels being descended from Milesius they would seem on investigation to have been a home grown order of men, bred among the Belgae-German colonies which after transplantation bore the modified appelations Fir Bolg and Gaileoin in their new homeland. Of all the Gaels, proudest in rank and for long centuries, most potent in authority, were the prosperous off shoots of the family of Conn-Ced-Chatach. For these and such others as were admitted into the patrician register of the Gaelic nobility, was specially invented the genealogical birth-badges emblematic of class privilege and of political prerogative which displays among its adornments the pseudo ancestral figures of Mil and Gaedhal Glas."

He continues: "Dazzled by the refulgent lustre of the Gael the literati of Leath Chuinn and Leath Mogh constructed a vain-glorious yet a puerile synthesis of the nation's primal stages of up-building. But among them were men of retentive memory who long preserved some genuine fragments of tradition, reminiscences of the period when Erinn's colonisers of the La Tene invasion, sank, disintegrated and disinherited under a forceful brood of their own begetting. That lusty brood, looking down from an imperial altitude on Erinn's vassal communities and growing ashamed of an origin which condemned them to kinship with masses of social inferiors, disowned their true parentage and evolved for themselves a genesis more consonant with the pride of a ruling class."

I have to acknowledge my indebtedness to all those authors on whose work I have drawn; to the Breifne Historical Society and the numerous contributors to its journal over many years, for permission to use excerpts from their articles. I am grateful to Mr W.A. Seaby, Senior Research Assistant of the Numismatics Department of the Ulster Museum for photographs of "The O'Reilly Money" and of the Cavan trade tokens, most of which are housed in the museum.

I have to acknowledge the supply of photographs, with permission to reproduce, from:

National Museum of Ireland
    Seal Matrix of Sir John O'Reilly
    Seal Matrix of Primate Hugh O'Reilly
    The Cavan Crozier
    The Breac Mogue
    The Cavan Brooch
    Flange Hilted Sword from Drumaura
    Polished Stone Axe Head from Blacklion
    Three faced Stone Head from Corleck

National Library of Ireland
    Kilmore Cathedral
    Kilnacrott
    Ross Castle, from a copy by W. Fraser, after a water colour by George Dunoyer (1864)

Wooden Image from bog at Rallaghan, Shercock
Portrait of General Philip Sheridan
University of Dublin, Trinity College Library (per Miss
Cruickshank, Director of Studies in Visual Arts)
Portraits of Colonel John O'Reilly and Don Alexan-
der O'Reilly (as a child). These portraits have been
identified and authenticated by Mr. O'Sullivan of
the Manuscript Department.

Heraldic Artists Ltd. College Green, Dublin.
Portrait of Don Alexander on horseback
Reproduction of the O'Reilly Coat of Arms

The British Museum
The Killanagh god
Cavan Sweat Houses

Victoria and Albert Museum
Seal matrix and profile of Cu-Connacht O'Reilly

Associated Book Publishers Ltd, New FetterLane, Lon-
don
Map of Ireland in 1014 showing boundaries of
Breifne

Mrs Ahern Getty
Photograph of the grave of Orwen and Sabina

I am indebted to Professor James Carney of the
Dublin Institute for Advanced Studies for permission to
quote from his "Genealogical History of the O'Reillys."
The genealogical tables in the appendix are compiled
from this work and from articles by the distinguished
scholar John O'Donovan in *Duffy's Magazine*, January–
February 1861, but only include such members as are
necessary to show the main lines of descent. Further details, together with a critical appraisement of all the

known O'Reilly genealogies, can be found in Professor Carney's book.

I am indebted to Mr B.E. O'Reilly of Noil Glenart Avenue Blackrock, County Dublin for permission to quote from "The O'Reillys of Templemills" by the late M.W. O'Reilly Esq. F.C.I.I..

The verses from "The Celts" are taken from the *Oxford Book of Irish Verse* published by the Clarendon Press, Walton St. Oxford who also publish *The Poetical Works of Byron*, from which the lines from "Don Juan" are taken. The verse "Salvete Flores Martyrum" is from *The Penguin Book of Latin Verse* published by Penguin Books Ltd. Harmondsworth, Middlesex. The verses from Browning's poem "Love among the Ruins" are taken from Volume II of his collected works published by the Unit Library Ltd. London. 1902.

Finally I have to acknowledge my deep gratitude to the late Dr. Philip O'Connell, M.Sc., F.R S.A.I., not only for the use of the valuable material contained in his book *The Diocese of Kilmore* but also for much help and guidance given in private correspondence. I am indebted to his brother Mr. Peter O'Connell of Croswater House, Carnacross, Kells County Meath for permission to quote freely from the book.

J.J. O'Reilly

Ferndown, Dorset

THE
HISTORY
OF
BREIFNE O'REILLY

CHAPTER I

Topography, Antiquities, Legends

> The Druid's altar and the Druid's creed
> We scarce can trace,
> There is not left an undisputed deed
> Of all your race,
> Save your majestic song, which hath their speed,
> And strength and grace;
> In that sole song, they live and love, and bleed—
> It bears them on through space.
>
> —"The Celts," Thomas D'Arcy Magee

Topography

The ancient territory of Breifne was co-extensive with the present counties of Cavan and Leitrim but included in addition a small portion of Meath and the barony of Carbery in Sligo.

In the tenth century the territory was divided into the two principalities of East Breifne or Breifne O'Reilly and West Breifne, Breifne O'Rourke. Breifne O'Reilly has a curious leg of mutton shape, with the large globular area in the south where it borders on County Meath, and a long narrow corridor running northwestwards where it is bounded by Upper Loch MacNean. Loch MacNean (Loc Mac N-En, i.e. the lake of the sons of En) extends between the present counties of Leitrim and

Fermanagh, and is partly situated in County Cavan.

In ancient times the whole area of Breifne was heavily wooded and watered, particularly in the broad southeastern portion which is a country of numerous small hillocks (druim), so that the county has been likened to a basket of eggs; a recent writer described it as a land of three plenties: loughs, hummocks and O'Reillys.

Near the southern border is Loch Ramor (Loch Muinreamhair, i.e. the Loch of the Fat Neck). The name is said to commemorate the pre-historic ancestor of a tribe which occupied that part of Breifne, and who were renowned for their physical strength. In the *Annals of the Four Masters* for the year "Anno Mundi" 2859 it is recorded that two lakes burst forth: Loch Dairbhreach (Derravaragh) in the present County Meath, and Loch Muinreamhair in Luigne, in Slieve Guaire.

To the west of Loch Ramor is Loch Sheelin, a much larger sheet of water covering some eight acres; it was closely associated with the fortunes of the O'Reilly clan. Over on the western margin is Loch Gowna, the source of the River Erne. Tradition says that the area it occupies was once a valley which was filled in by building a dam across it. The dam is said to have been constructed as early as the century before Christ and was the work of an engineer named Maoin Dubh (Black Maon) who resided at Tullyvin (Tulach Mhaoin, i.e. Maon's Hill). He also constructed the Black Pig's Dyke or Race which marked the boundary of ancient Ulster; he was the son of Conal Cearnach, one of the Red Branch knights.

Conal Cearnach lived during the La Tene period which was from about 300 B.C. to 100 A.D. He was said to have been a cousin of the great Ulster champion Cu-Chullain; indeed in the heroic sagas he was regarded as second only to Cu-Chullain himself. He seems to have travelled widely outside Ireland and there is a story that on his return from overseas he was recounting

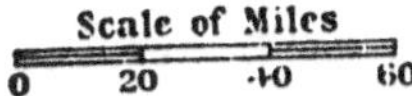

An Eleventh Century map showing the subkingdom of Breifne; (shown as "brefni" on map).

3

his adventures in the House of the Red Branch, in the course of which he said that his most outstanding experience occurred in a city of the Eastern world where he came upon a crowd on a hill, surrounding three crosses on which were fastened three malefactors whom they were about to crucify. Looking at the face of one of them Conal felt that his punishment could not possibly be justified. He pushed his way through to the front of the crowd and in a rage drew his sword, prepared to drive the rabble off and rescue the condemned man. But as he stood there a drop of blood from the crucified fell on his breast and at that moment, said Conal, "I know not why, but all rage departed from my heart."

Cu-Chullain, eventually, was killed and beheaded on the plain of Muirthemne near the present town of Dundalk. Shortly afterwards Conal Cearnach came to Tara to find out the truth about the killing; there he came on two young men playing hurley, and the ball they were playing with was a human head. Conal asked them why the game was being played like that and they replied that Cu-Chullain had been slain by the men of Ireland and that this was his head. "Your heads with his," said Conal and promptly beheaded them both.

According to legend, Conal killed the Breifne champion Belcu and was himself killed through the treachery of Maeve, Queen of Connacht, whose husband he had slain at her instigation. He fled from her domain but was followed by three of her retainers, the Ruad-Choin (Red Heads), who overtook him on the confines of Magh Sleacht and slew him at Ath-na-Mianna on the River Graine (now the Woodford River). Ath-na-Mianna means "the ford of the miners where they washed the iron ore." The place is now the site of the town of Ballyconnell (Beul-atha-Conaill, i.e. The Ford Mouth of Conal). Tradition points out his burial mound on Ballyheady mountain south of Ballyconnell, and it is at least an interesting coincidence that during excavations in the area in 1932 a male skeleton was unearthed. It has been suggested that the place named Tomkinroad near Belturbet most probably signifies the burial place (Tuaim) of the Ruadh Choin who murdered Conal.[1]

There is a curious legend associated with Loch Gowna. It is the story of a young girl who went to a well for water and forgot to replace the cover. As a result the evil spirit of the well was released in the shape of a calf which chased her over the fields until she came in the path of a mower who cut her legs off with his scythe, whereupon the calf disappeared. Thus Loch Gowna got its name, Loch Gamhna, "The Lake of the Calf."

In the central part of this wide southeastern part is an enormous tangled area of land and water known as Loch Uachtair, an area in which, even today, it is only too easy to lose one's way. The lake is believed to have got its name from being the upper (uachter) lake on the River Erne; though properly speaking, Loch Gowna has that distinction.

From the region of Loch Uachtair a long narrow corridor runs northwestward, the landscape becoming more sparse and isolated, and in its upper portion, more mountainous, as it proceeds. On its northern side it marches with Fermanagh over the summit of Cuilcagh (the Chalky) mountain, 2,188 feet high, and on its southern flank with Leitrim, over Slieve-na-Killa (Sliabh na Cille, i.e. Church Mountain), 1793 feet. In this region are the headwaters of the Shannon River, a small pool called the Lugnashinna or Shannon Pot. It is the exit of an underground river coming from the north or northeast, in both of which directions a few miles away, streams sink underground. All this area is predominently limestone honeycombed with subterranean passages. Several streams come down the northern face of Cuilcagh and vanish underground as soon as they reach solid rock.

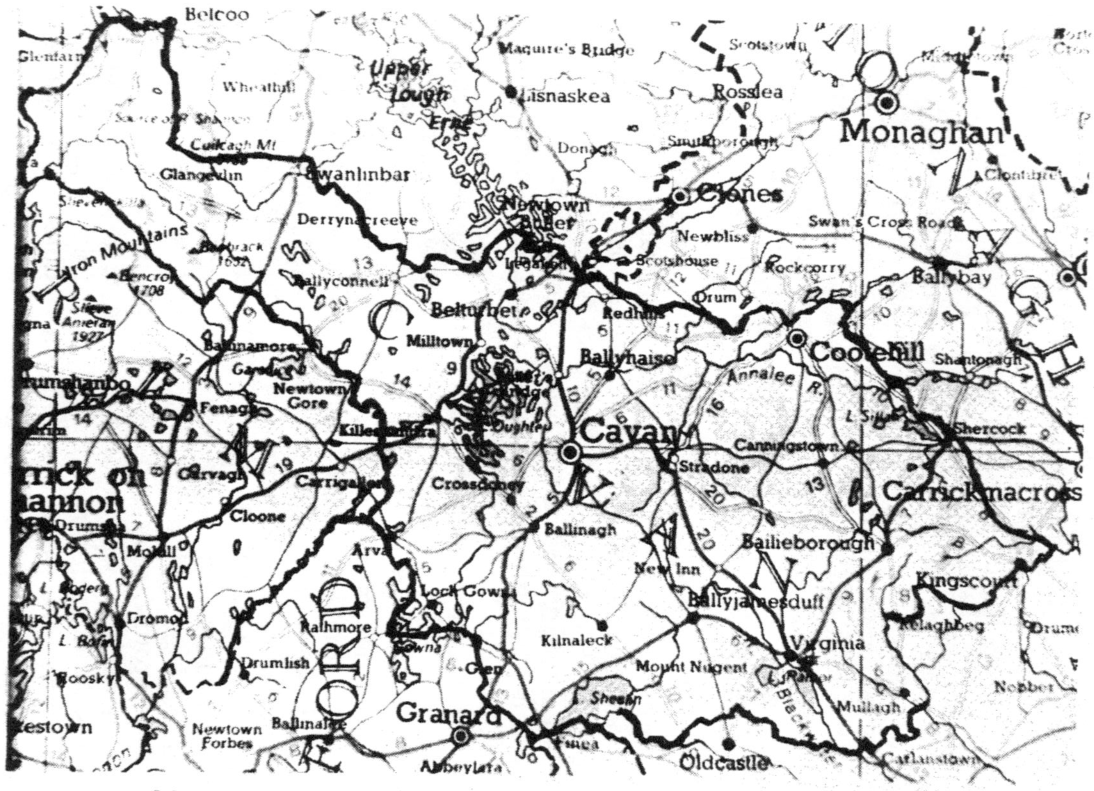

Map of present-day County Cavan, Ireland. (Based on the Ordance Survey by permission of the government Permit No. 2224).

All this northwest area is steeped in history and may fairly be called the cradle of Breifne.

Nothing is really known as to how the name Breifne originated. The earliest form of the name was Breibne; in the Annals of Ulster the slaughter of the men of Breibne is recorded under the year 882.A.D. It has been suggested that the name is a survival from pre-Celtic times commemorating the title of some eponymous ancestor of its pre-Celtic race. The Dinnsencus derives it from Breifne the daughter of Beoan MacBethaig who disputed the territory with the Fomorian chieftain, Regan.

With regard to the early inhabitants of Breifne, as of Ireland as a whole, tradition says that there were five early invasions of Ireland, all originating in the Mediterranean basin. The first two colonisations were led by Partholan and Nemed, and although these names take us back to the dim legendary epoch it is interesting to note that the name of Partholan is associated with Glenade in County Leitrim, which in Irish is Gleann Eada, the glen of jealousy, said to have its origin in the jealousy between Partholan and his wife Dealgnait about the prehistoric settlements in that area.

Some of the Nemedians returned to the Mediterranean area where they were reduced into slavery and set to carry loads of earth in bags from the plains to enrich the vineyards on the hillsides. For this reason they were called the Firbolgs or "men of the leathern sack." Some time later the Firbolgs returned to Ireland; they are the earliest inhabitants of whom we have any real knowledge. In Breifne they settled principally in the area around the Erne basin and for this reason were known as the Erenachs or Ernea.

These Firbolgs are believed to have been the builders of the crannoga or lake dwellings, the remains of which are found in Cavan, Leitrim, and Fermanagh. These crannoga are of great antiquity; some which have been excavated were built in the Bronze Age and rebuilt in the early Christian era. The crannoge is an artificial structure, an island built on a foundation of wooden piles driven into the bed of the lake and filled in with stones, rubble, peat, and brushwood so that eventually a firm base is achieved, on which a dwelling is erected. It is because of the large amount of timber used in their construction that they are called crannoga, from the Irish Crann, a tree. They were evidently fortified dwellings strategically placed at some distance from the shore, to which they were sometimes connected by an underwater causeway.

Although most known examples of these structures were entirely artificial in origin, occasionally advantage was taken of a small island or rock as a foundation. Numerous examples of crannoga were to be seen in Loch Erne in quite recent times.[2]

The Firbolgs were a low-statured, dark-skinned, dark-eyed people. Some forty years after their arrival a new body of invaders arrived, the Tuatha de Danann. They also were of Nemedian stock but whereas the Firbolgs on their departure from Ireland had settled in Attica, these others had gone to Thrace and there learnt the art of magic from the Greeks. When Greece was overrun by the Syrians these Nemedians fled to Scandinavia, from whence they came to Ireland. They were a tall, fair, blue-eyed race renowned for their skill in magic, and very soon they were contending with the Firbolgs for possession of the land. One of the most momentous battles took place at Magh Turadh (Moytura) in the area between Lochs Corrib and Mask.

In these early times Breifne was rich in minerals particularly gold and iron and the Tuatha de Danann were highly skilled workers in the latter metal. There is an interesting sidelight in connection with the battle of Moytura. There is ample evidence that iron was worked in Breifne from the earliest times, indeed it is from this activity that Slieve-an-Iarainn (the Iron Mountain) on the eastern shore of Loch Allen on the Cavan-Leitrim border, gets its name. In an early account of the battle the manufacture of javelins by the de Danann smith, Gaibhlen, is described in detail: "At the northern end of Magh Sleacht in the district of Glangevlin was sited the forge of Guibnen or Gaibhlen, the Tuatha de Danann smith; he withdrew the red hot bar from the furnace and having formed it on the anvil, produced in quick time the finished article."[3]

Glangevlin gorge lies in the barony of Tullyhaw close to the border between the two Breifnes. At the southeastern end it is entered at Bellavally Gap. The distinguished antiquarian John O'Donovan found it recorded that "the immortal glen takes its name from the famous cow called Glas Gaibhlen which belonged to the smith of that name. This cow supplied all the glen with milk and when passing out of it her udder was so vastly large that it formed the gap between the mountains Cuilcagh and Slieve-an-Iarainn called Bellavally Gap (Beal a Bhealaigh, i.e. The Mouth of the Pass)."[4]

The final wave of invasion came in 350 B.C. with the arrival of the Milesians. According to the *Leabar Gabala* (The Book of Invasions) the three sons of King Milesius of Spain, Heremon, Heber, and Ir, came to Ireland about the time of Alexander the Great and from them were descended all the royal clans of later Ireland. To this day wherever Irish is spoken the story of the "Meela Spaunya" is remembered, and to be of the old Milesian race is an honourable distinction.[5]

The Milesians quickly routed the Tuatha de Danann who passed into legend as the Sidhe, the fairy folk; the Firbolgs however, were made of sterner stuff; fierce battles took place in Breifne between themselves and the Milesians, contending for supremacy. On one occasion the defeated Firbolgs invited the Milesian kings to a banquet at Mac Dareo's hostel in Magh Cro and mur-

The high mound of Moybolge where in A.D. 56 the defeated Milesians were buried after the battle of Magh Bolg.

dered them there. In A.D. 56 the Milesians suffered a further defeat at the battle of Magh Bolg in East Breifne where they were practically annihilated; a high mound there indicates where they were buried. Twenty years later, in 76 A.D. under King Tuathal Teachtmar whose father, Fiachra Finnolaidh was slain at Magh Bolg, the Milesian rule was restored.

Antiquities

There are no first class historical remains in Breifne; the constant vicious onslaughts of the English during the sixteenth century destroyed the majority of the churches and castles, and those which survived were left to crumble into ruin when their owners were evicted during the Plantation. On the other hand, there are numerous archaeological remains; crannoga, cairns, stone circles, pillar stones, and bullauns are scattered all around. Paricularly in the neighbourhood of Loch Ramor there are the dolmens or cromlechs so called, built by the neolithic inhabitants prior to 2000 B.C. The terms cromlechs, giants graves, or Druid's altars applied to these structures are inaccurate; they are properly called

10

Dolmen of the secondary type found at Carrickacroy, Cavan, Ireland.

dolmens, a term deriving from the Breton "daelmaen" meaning a stone table.

The dolmen is a structure with stone uprights supporting a massive capstone; there are two types, depending on the method of their construction. In the primary type one end of the capstone rests on the earth or on a flat stone slab while the other end is supported by the uprights. In the secondary type the raised capstone rests entirely on the uprights. Several examples of both types are described in detail by O'Connell,[6] notably at Ballaghanea near Loch Ramor, at Mullagh in the townland of Raffony and in Crosserlough parish. In the townland of Aghawee near Drumreilly is an example of the secondary type which in O'Connell's time was in a good state of preservation; it consisted of two large capstones resting on five uprights slanting into one

11

another. At Duffcastle near Ballyjamesduff there is a dolmen of primary type which has as a capstone a huge boulder, a glacial erratic utilised for the purpose, with one end resting on a flat stone and the other on an upright about five feet in height. At Carrickacroy between Crosserlough and Kilnaleck, near the summit of the hill there is a dolmen of secondary type but the capstone has been long since displaced.

O'Connell suggests that in most cases the collapse of the capstone has resulted from the crude excavations of treasure seekers in search of the ubiquitous "crock of gold." Elsewhere, in cases where dolmens have been carefully explored, traces of primitive burials have been discovered showing that they were constructed as tombs by the neolithic people. He considers that the dolmen was a tomb in a double sense; it contained the body of the chieftain and furthermore was understood to continue as the place of residence of his spirit. According to primitive ideas the spirit was destined to a perpetual existence in the tomb prepared for it.[7]

Some objects pertaining to later periods have been discovered from time to time. A wooden figure, now in the National Museum of Ireland, was found in a bog at Ralaghan, Shercock, in 1930. The figure, which lay under three to four feet of turf, is made of yew and stands about three feet eight inches high. Dr. Adolf Mahr, then Keeper of Irish Antiquities in the Museum thus described it:

There were no arms though the body is rather carefully curved. The hole in the centre of the body, obviously intended for the insertion of a male organ, is drilled, and the whole area is somewhat accentuated. The projection at the base, I am told, was inserted into a socket cut in a block shaped pedestal about a foot square in area; it is now lost. The figure lay on its face. Nothing else has been found previously or since. A few figures of more or less similar workmanship are known from different countries, including Great

12

Wooden figure found in a bog at Ralaghan, Shercock, Ireland, in 1930. Originally fitted on pedestal. Also note hole where separate male sex organ carving went.

Britain, Denmark, and Germany. The female idol from Bal-lachulish is the nearest British parallel.[8]

About 1935 some men digging rabbits out of a bur-row in the townland of Drumaura in the parish of Drung, discovered a bronze sword. "The sword belongs to the group generally called flange hilted; the blade which is comparatively wide near the tip is pointed, oval in cross section. The cutting edges are still quite sharp. The sword is 54.9cm long, 5cm wide across the shoulder and its maximum thickness is 6mm.

"In general, flange hilted swords such as this, can be dated to what is known as the Late Bronze Age, that is roughly speaking, a period after 1000 B.C. It is as yet impossible to say how long swords of this type lasted in Ireland. In some areas they may have been replaced by iron swords or bronze swords of another type, by 500 or 400 B.C., while in other districts they may have con-tinued in use practically down to the time of Christ. The most that can be said therefore, of the Drumaura sword in the present state of our knowledge is that it is from 2500 to 3000 years old."[9]

Another find was a stone axe head turned up by a farmer near Bailieboro while digging a drain in a field. "Dimensions were: length 14.5cm.; width at the cutting edge 7cm.; at the butt 4.5cm.; maximum thickness 2.5cm. Several such axe heads have been found in the Loch Uachtair area. When in use the axe head was mounted in a wooden handle by being passed through a hole cut in the end of the wood. As these weapons are found so often on riverside sites it would seem that some of them were used by a people who camped for short spells in the summer months beside stream and lakes for sea-sonal fishing. They are neolithic in type but the discov-ery of stone axe heads on Bronze Age and early historic sites indicates that such objects were made and used into the early Christian centuries."[10]

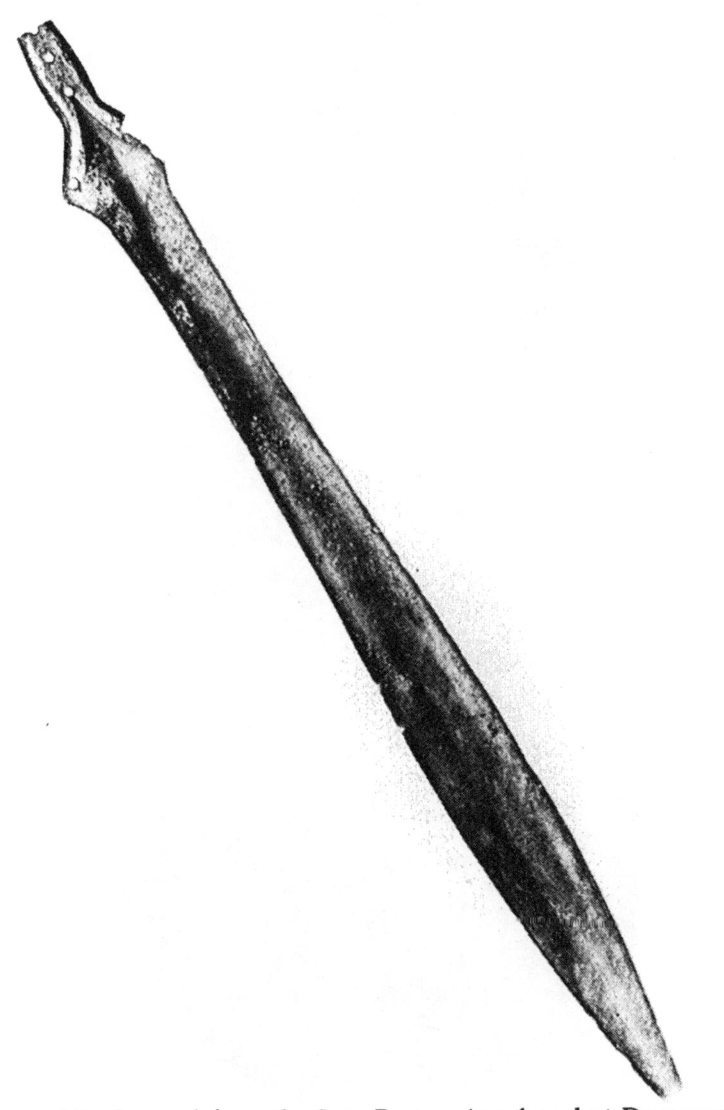

Flange hilted sword from the Late Bronze Age found at Drumaura, Cavan, Ireland in 1935.

Polished Bronze Age stone axe head, found near Bailieboro, at Bracklin, Cavan, Ireland.

Three-faced stone head found at Corleck, Cavan, Ireland. Ascribed to Iron Age times, these have been found commonly over wide areas of Europe.

A curious object found at Corleck is a three-faced head, now in the National Museum. Nothing is known about it other than it is generally believed to be related to a series of three-faced and two-faced stone heads which have a wide distribution in Europe and are ascribed to Iron Age times.

In pre-historic times Ireland was very rich in gold, possibly the richest country in the world, and Breifne is particularly rich in gold finds including gold brooches. The Cavan Brooch, now in the National Museum, is in silver gilt, beautifully worked; the external diameter of the ring is 4¼ inches. A replica of this brooch was presented to Queen Victoria, since then it has more often been called "The Queen's Brooch." There is some doubt whether this brooch was actually found in Cavan but other brooches of the same type, the Virginia Brooch, the Day Brooch, and the Shantemon Brooch, certainly were. The latter was picked up some seventy years ago on Shantemon Hill not far from the mystic five stones known as Finn Mac Coul's Fingers which crown its summit. The brooch is not merely the oldest connected with Breifne, but is one of the most ancient objects of its kind known about in Ireland.[11]

Brooches were much worn by men in Ireland; the Brehon Law prescribed that the sons of higher kings were to have their mantles fastened with one in gold and the sons of a Tuath, with one in silver.

Shantemon is the hill on which the O'Reilly chiefs were inaugurated. The five standing stones are believed to be Druidical remains.

Sweat Houses in Breifne

The following account of these interesting structures is given by P. Richardson.

"Although sweat houses are comparatively rare in Ulster, in two districts there are considerable groups,

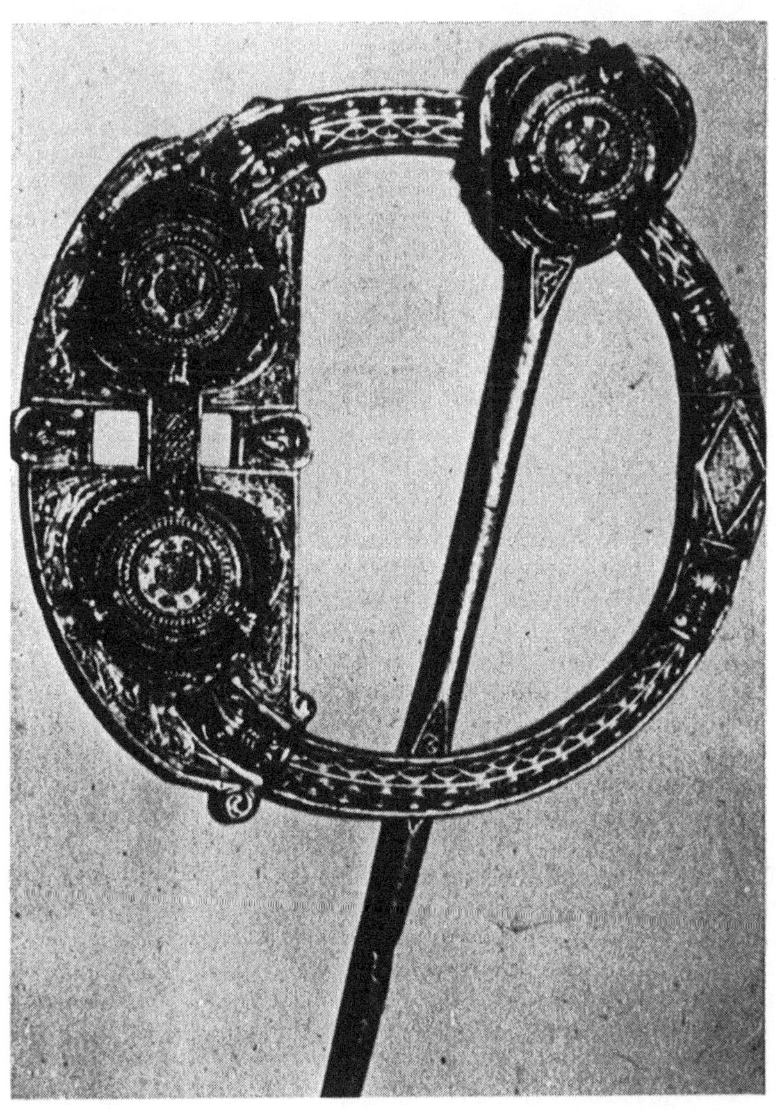

The Cavan-Brooch, Silver gilt. The Brehon Law prescribed brooches like this be used to fasten the mantles of the sons of higher kings.

Finn Mc Coul's Fingers, Druid remains atop Shantemon Hill, Cavan, Ireland. Where O'Reilly chiefs were inaugurated.

around Carrickmore (Tyrone), and in the extreme west of County Cavan. Of this latter group I have visited twenty-five and have taken measurements and photographs. No one can remember their being built. I would indeed be tempted to suggest that the Danes, raiding up the Shannon, introduced a custom known also in Finland. But it cannot be proved that the Irish sweat houses are not earlier than the Danish invasions; and the two Ulster groups lie in somewhat inaccessible mountain districts, whither foreign influences would have been slow to penetrate.

''Most elderly people can remember the Cavan sweat houses in use about forty years ago (prior to 1939). They seem to have been abandoned then; no one could tell me why, but the reason may have been the dispensaries then being founded, and that the scientific

20

Cavan sweat houses. Turf fires burnt in these houses for several days. Then the ashes were cleaned out and while still hot, men and women entered them to take the "cure." Some were used as late as forty years ago.

world of that date was more inclined to despise popular medicine than it is today. One would not expect superstitions to be attached to objects remembered to have been of general utility; only in one case, at Port, did the owner tell me that he would not go near the spot at night.

"All my information agreed as to the method of use. Turf fires were lighted in the sweat house; sometimes the turf had to be carried up the mountain in panniers on the backs of donkeys. At Corrakeeldrum five loads were required. The fire burnt for several days; different women would be responsible for the turf and for tending the fire each day. At the end of this time both walls and floor of the sweat house had become thoroughly heated. The ashes were then raked out, the floor was swept, and green rushes were spread thickly over it. The people then removed their clothes before they entered the sweat house. In some cases the clothes were used to block the doorway. I was told that most of the sweat houses, for instance, Tullynamoyle, were used in summer; at Moneen the cure took place in the autumn. At least two people, often more, sometimes as many as six, entered at once, lest one should become dizzy. After sitting for about an hour inside, the sufferers bathed in a stream, which usually flows only a few yards from the sweat house; they then wrapped themselves up well and went home to bed.

"The sweat houses were used sometimes by men and sometimes by women. I was told at Corraquigley and at Tullynamoyle that they were regarded as a cure for rheumatism or 'pains'. Many old people remembered when each townland had its sweat house. They are less than half a mile apart in Legnagrow, and only a few hundred yards at Corcashel. My information at Moneen described how drifts of women could be seen going to the sweat houses.

"The sweat houses are normally beehive constructions, usually with roof partially corbelled and closed by one or two slabs. They are sometimes built into the side of a hill. Their corbelled roofs would require counter-weighting on the outside, so they are often covered with earth or turf; despite this precaution the roof has often fallen in. The walls are built of stone blocks roughly fitted. The rectangular splitting of the limestone of this district facilitates such building. Chinks were often filled with clay or mortar. The doorway is always low, and normally spanned by one or two lintel blocks. There is also a chimney, roughly constructed in the wall. Sometimes the floor is paved. They are usually situated near water."[12]

MAGH SLEACHT

And we are here as on a darkling plain,
Swept with confused alarms of struggle and flight,
When ignorant armies clash by night.

—Matthew Arnold

Throughout the early centuries Magh Sleacht was the scene of sacrificial slaughter and sanguinary battles between the O'Reillys on the one hand, and the O'Rourkes and O'Connors on the other. The name Magh Sleacht has been variously interpreted as "The Plain of Adoration," "The Plain of Genuflexions," and "The Plain of Prostration". There are reasons for thinking that the latter may be the more correct. Magh Sleacht was the site of the chief pagan idol of Ireland—Cromm Cruaich (Cromm of the Rick), said to have been introduced into the country by the Firbolgs. In those early times the name of Magh Sleacht was applied only to the area surrounding the shrine of Cromm but later it covered a much wider area stretching from the Woodford River in the east up to Cuilcagh mountain in the north and Slieve an Iarain in the west. Dalton[13] described it as a large rhomboidal area in the southeast of Tullyhaw barony. Though presenting everywhere crumpled and twisted elevations of surface and no part of it could be described as flat, yet it appeared low lying in contrast with the towering Slieve Russell along its northern margin and the long ranges of Slieve an Iarain which dominate it from the west.

The actual site of Cromm's statue, covered in gold and surrounded by twelve lesser gods covered in brass, has been shown by Dalton to have been within an elliptical rath on the summit of the hill of Derryragh, locally called Darraugh, in the parish of Templeport, which is in the eastern part of Tullyhaw barony, south of Slieve Russell and southeast of Cuilcagh.

Being the chief idol of the country a great highway led from the royal court at Tara to the southern shore of Lake Garadice south of Derryragh. Here, at the narrowest part of the lake, the pilgrims embarked on their journey "over the water, chanting loud lamentations which reverberated in the surrounding hills." Hence the contemporary name of the lake, Guthard, meaning "loud voice."

It was said the people used to sacrifice their children to this idol to obtain fair weather and fertility for their crops. "It was milk and corn they asked from it in exchange for their children," says the tract called *Dinnsenchus*—"how great was their horror and their moaning."

According to the *Dinnsenchus*, although human sacrifices were eventually abandoned, worship continued in a manner which entailed severe bodily suffering. "They all prostrated themselves before him [Cromm] so that the tops of their foreheads and the gristle of their noses and the caps of their knees and the ends of their elbows broke, and three fourths of the men of Erin perished at these prostrations."[14]

The name Cromm is derived from the old Irish name for thunder; the rolling peals of thunder around Cuilcagh and Slieve Russell were, to the terrified worshippers the angry voice of their Thunder God.

> Long long ago beyond the misty space
> Of twice a thousand years, mighty
> In Erin old there dwelt a race
> Taller than Roman spears—
> Cromah their Day-God and their thunderer
> Made morning and eclipse.

—"The Celts," Thomas D'Arcy McGee

Notes

1. *Kilmore*. Browne & Nolan. Richview Press. Clonskeagh, Dublin.4.

2. Maire & Liam de Paor. *Early Christian Ireland.* London, Thames & Hudson. 1958.

3. Cath Magh Tured. *Revue Celtique.* Vol. XII.

4. J.A.S. Vol. III. pp 57 et seq.

5. Edmund Curtis. *A History of Ireland.* Associated Book Publishers Ltd. 11 New Fetter Lane. London. EC4P 4EE.

6. B.A.S. Vol. III. No. 1. 1927. O'Connell.

7. Opus Cit.

8. *Antiquity,* Vol. IV, 1930.

9. *Breifne.* Vol. I. No. 3, 1960. Joseph Raftery. M.A.D. Phil. Keeper Irish Antiquities. National Museum.

10. *Breifne.* Vol. I. No. 4. 1961. Thomas Barron.

11. B.A.S. Vol. II. No. 1. 1923.

12. U.J.A. 1939. P. Richardson.

13. R.I.A. Proc. John P. Dalton. M.A.; M.R.I.A.; Sec. C. Vol. XXXVI. No.4. 1922.

14. *Revue Celtique.* Vol. XVI. p 35.

CHAPTER II

The Advent of Christianity

Discede, Christus hic est,
Hic Christus est, liquesce!
Signum quod ipse nosti
Damnat tuam catervam.

Prudentius

Saint Patrick came to Ireland in A.D.432 and after his encounter with the Druids on the Hill of Slane established a strong body of Christian converts, but he soon became aware of the mighty influence wielded by the national deity, Cromm Cruaich, and realised that if his mission was to be successful he would have to destroy this idol. Accordingly in A.D.435 he set out for the great plain of Magh Sleacht, choosing a time when a great concourse of pilgrims, including the High King Laoghaire, was making its way there from Tara.

We are told in the *Tripartite Life* that St. Patrick went over the water to Magh Sleacht, a place in which was the chief idol of Ireland, namely Cenn Cruaich, covered with silver and gold and twelve other idols covered with brass about him.[1]

The *Memoir of Tirechan* states that Saint Patrick sailed "over the water called Guthard," now known as Lake Garadice and landed on the opposite shore, about half a mile from Cromm's shrine.[2] The *Tripartite Life* continues:

When he drew near the idol he raised up his hand to put
Jesus' staff upon it, and reached it not, but . . . its right side,
for to the south was its face, namely, to Tara; and the mark of
the staff still remains on its left side, and yet the staff did not
move out of Patrick's hand. And the earth swallowed up the
twelve other images as far as their heads, and they stand thus
in token of the miracle. And he cursed the demon and expelled him into hell. And Patrick summoned all with King
Laoghaire. These are they who adored the idol, and all saw
him, namely the demon, and they feared they would perish
unless Patrick should cast him into hell.[3]

Following this spectacular miracle, St. Patrick
founded a church called Domnach Magh Sleacht, plac-
ing in charge of it his disciple and kinsman, Methbran.
Needless to say he made a large number of converts
whom he baptised at a nearby well; but King Laoghaire,
while he showed every tolerance to the new religion and
extended his protection to its missionaries, refused to
accept it himself. ''For,'' said he ''Niall [of the Nine Hos-
tages] my father did not permit me to believe, but required that I should be buried in the top of Temrach like
men standing up in war.''[4] It was Niall who, on one of
his raids on Britain, captured Patrick and brought him as
a slave to Ireland. Niall reigned from 379 to 405 A.D.;
the wording of his admonition to Laoghaire lends some
support to the suggestion that Christianity was known
in Ireland before the arrival of Saint Patrick.
Cormac Mac Art High King of Ireland from 254 to
266 A.D. was one of the wisest of the Milesian kings.
Amongst other things he is said to have introduced the
first water mills into Ireland. He spent many years
abroad with his fleet and doubtless was aware of the
new religious teaching. Indeed, according to the Four
Masters his Christianity was the cause of his death.
Their entry under the year A.D. 266 records:

Cormac the son of Art, son of Con, after having been forty
years in the government of Ireland, died at Sletty, the bone of

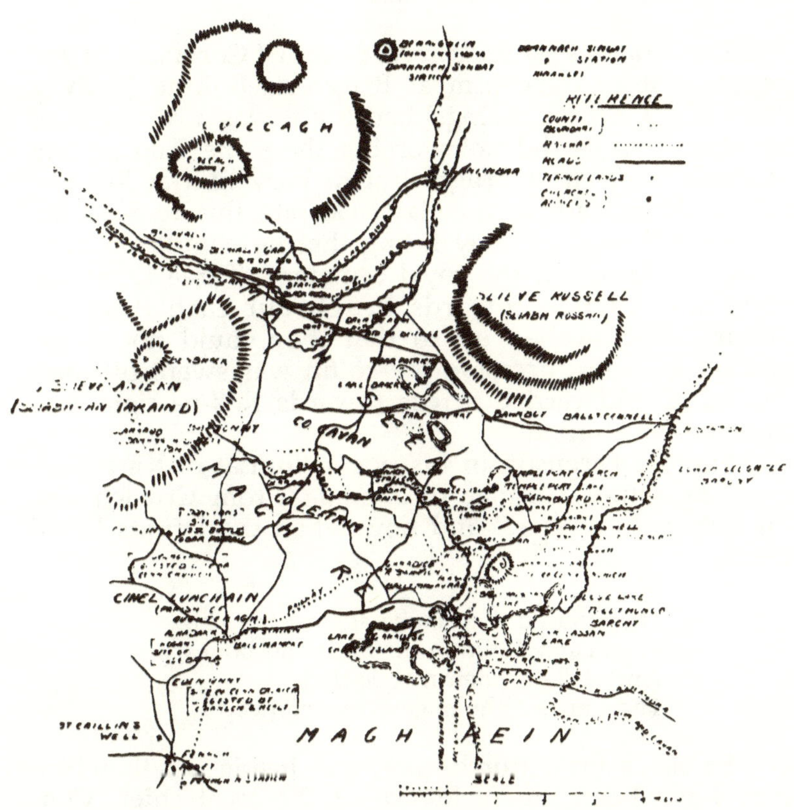

Map showing territories of Magh Sleacht and Mach Rein.

a salmon having stuck in his throat through the Shreeva whom Mailgenn the chief Druid induced to attack him after Cormac had turned from the Druids to the adoration of God. Wherefore a demon attacked him at the instigation of the Druids and gave him a painful death.[5]

The *Seanchas na Roilc* records that "Cormac told his people not to bury him at Brugh-na-Boinne [resting place of the Milesian kings] because it was a cemetery of idolators, for he did not worship the same God as any of those interred at Brugh, but to bury him at Ros-na-righ with his face to the East. Despite this request his followers thought it only fitting that he should be hon-ourably interred in the royal cemetery. Three times his body was carried towards Brugh but each time the Boyne River swelled up so that they could not cross, and on the third occasion the coffin was swept off their shoulders and carried across towards Ros-na-righ, and there he was buried."

Samuel Ferguson in his poem "Burial of King Cor-mac" tells how Cormac disowned "Crom Cruaich and his sub-gods twelve," and how when the Druids heard this:

> They loosed their curse against the king,
> They cursed him in his flesh and bones;
> And daily in their mystic ring
> They turned the maledictive stones.[6]

Patrick's first church was built inside a rath which may have been the residence of the local chief. Cen-turies later a modern church, Kilnavart (Cill na bfeart, i.e. the Church of the Graves) was built on the same spot.

The large number of holy wells dedicated to Saint Patrick testify to the wide area of Breifne which he cov-ered and the length of time he spent there until he was satisfied that Christianity was firmly established in the territory. Although not mentioned in the *Tripartite Life* there is strong traditional support for the belief that he spent some time in the eastern corner of Breifne, particularly in the neighbourhood of Moybolge, an area somewhat indefinite in extent lying close to the Meath border.

The saint's object in visiting Moybolge was to destroy a pagan deity which, though not enjoying the national veneration accorded to Crom Cruaich, had nevertheless a strong local following. The traditional story of the miraculous destruction of this deity is derived from a legend which is in itself wildly fantastic but may have a basis of fact. O'Connell gives it as follows:

The story is that Saint Patrick journeyed into Moybolge, the plain of the Firbolg race, and having made a number of converts, erected a church there. On a Sunday morning when the people were gathering to hear Mass, a beautiful young woman called Geargáin was walking towards the church, fasting, with the intention of receiving Holy Communion; on the way she met a horseman whom she asked to hand her some blackberries which were growing on top of a fence. She ate them and was immediately blown into four pieces which were scattered to the four winds.[7]

O'Connell suggests that the basis of the legend is that there was a local pagan female deity, the Cailleach Geargáin (Cailleac, i.e. an old woman) and that she was regarded as the special protectoress of the Firbolg race inhabiting Magh Bolg. The pagan ancestors of the Clan Mac Garrigan who ruled over the district would have regarded her as their own special divinity. Following the destruction of the idol a church was built on the summit of the moat of Moybolge, traditionally regarded as the burial place of the Cailleach.

On one of the islands in nearby Loch Ramor, now known as Woodward's Island, it is believed that an ecclesiastical foundation was established by two of Saint

Patrick's missionaries, S.S. Brandubh and Coluim. Later, in mediaeval times there was a monastery or church there, founded from the Augustinian Abbey of Kells. At some early date the church was plundered by a band of robbers and the monks were slain; the robbers then quarreled amongst themselves about the division of the spoils and a great battle was fought in the neighbouring district of Ballanea; a hillock here, known as Cnoc Fola (The Hill of Blood) is said to mark the scene of the conflict.

The Annals of the Four Masters under the year 845 A.D. records the demolition of the island by Maelseachlainn, king of Meath, against a great crowd of the sons of death (i.e. malefactors) of the Luighne and Gailenga who were plundering the district at the instigation of the foreigners (i.e. the Norsemen); and they were destroyed by him.

A map of 1609 shows the island with a rectangular church building, unroofed and with pointed gables; this church appears to have been built sometime during the fourteenth century. In the late seventeenth century it was demolished by a Colonel Woodward who used the materials to build an ornate mansion for himself. Colonel Woodward was himself demolished in May 1726 when during the course of a royal birthday celebration an over-loaded cannon exploded prematurely, killing the Colonel and several other people.

On the southern shores of Loch MacNean are the ruins of the ancient church of Killinagh (Cill Laigne, the church of Laigne or the church of the Leinsterman). According to local tradition the church was founded jointly by S.S. Brigid and Laigne early in the sixth century.

Professor Davies, under the title "Killinagh Church and Cromm Cruaich,"[8] has recorded a curious local tradition that at one time there was a partially carved standing stone near to the church which was later moved to a site about two miles to the east, in the townland of Drum-

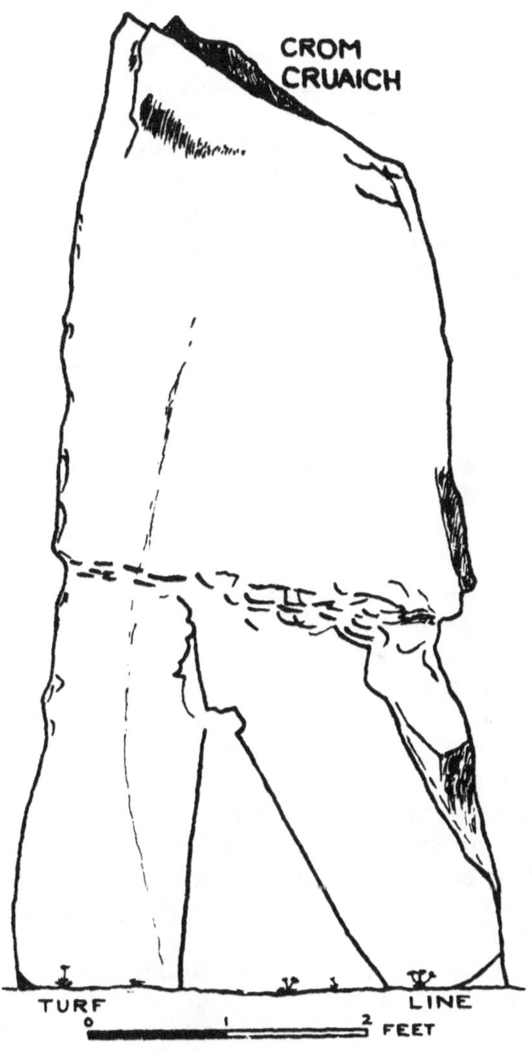

The Killinagh God. This stone near the ancient church in Killinagh is presumed to be an idol to Cromm Cruaich.

coo near Belcoo, to conceal it from zealous Christian missionaries. Local people say that the stone was once gilded, and was in fact the idol Cromm Cruaich at which Saint Patrick threw his staff splitting the idol and causing a fissure which may still be seen at the top of the west side of the stone. Professor Davies describes the stone as standing nearly seven feet high above the turf; it is of trapezoidal section, the back side being narrow and uncarved. The upper part of the front or north face is also rough but at rather less than three feet from the turf a pick cut depression on the north and west and extending six inches round on the south side, marks apparently, a girdle; the pick marks are clearly visible. Below this, raised in flat relief half an inch high may be traced the forms of two footless legs and, apparently, the tassel of a girdle or kilt between them.

Of course, having regard to what we know of the situation of Magh Sleacht it is obvious that this could not be the famous Cromm Cruaich. Davies conjectures that this was a local idol to which the name of Cromm Cruaich became attached.

In the outer face of the north wall of the ruined church there are two curious heart-shaped stones with rough borders within which are smooth fields raised about a quarter of an inch in relief and approximately of the same shape as the stones. Davies suggests that they have no connection with the church but were built into the wall to preserve them. Not far from the church is a group of three erratic boulders known as Saint Brigid's "cursing stone." On the top of the largest boulder there is a smooth round stone lying in a smooth depression, surrounded by a circle of nine similar stones each set in a separate bullaun or socket. It was said that these stones were formerly turned in their sockets by persons who wished to bring a curse on someone who had injured them, the condition being that if the curse fell the accusation was just, but that otherwise it recoiled on the

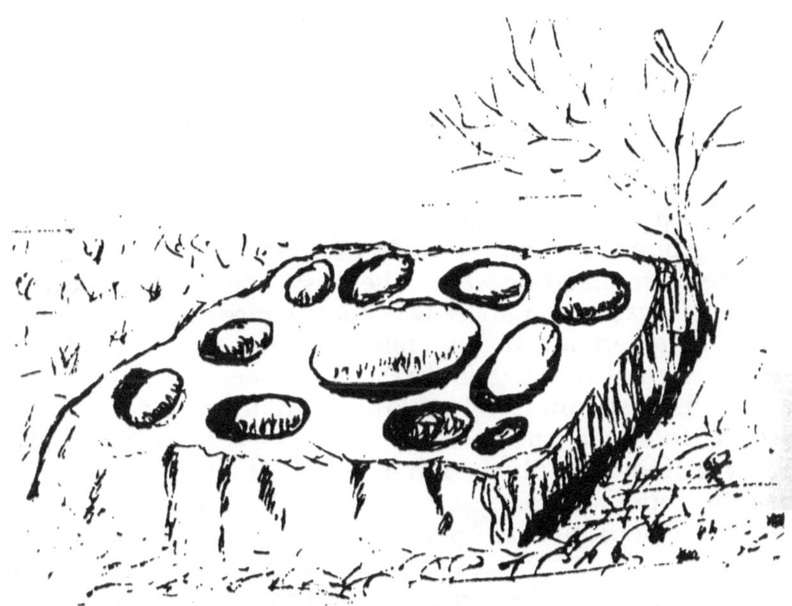

Saint Brigid's "cursing stone" in the ancient church at Killinagh. The argument is over whether it is a cursing stone or a village mill.

head of the person who invoked it. Davies is of opinion that the so-called cursing stone was a pagan altar and that the heart shaped stones stood, one on either side of it. O'Connell gives an entirely different account and explanation of this bullaun.[9] It was, he says, a unique example of a quern, the earliest form of mill for crushing grain. It is made of red sandstone, stands about three feet high and measures about five feet nine inches from east to west and five feet two inches from north to south. On its upper surface are nine cavities, eight of which are arranged irregularly around the margin with one, the largest, in the centre. Each hollow is filled with a loose stone oval in shape. The bullaun was in reality the village mill. He quotes Bennett and Elton[10] referring to the Killinagh bullaun as "one of the most impressive

35

monuments of its curious class remaining in the country." They concluded that "it is nothing more than the common mealing stone of the early settlements on the site of Killinagh at which, if necessary, eight women could grind together the grain for their families."

John O'Donovan in his Ordnance Survey name-books refers to the church of Killinagh and its ancient burial ground. He expressed himself at a loss to account for the form Laighneach in the Irish spelling but adds that the local explanation was that it meant the church of the Leinsterman. In his Tullyhaw letter he relates that "of St. Leney nothing is now remembered but that he was a Leinsterman who, falling in love with Saint Brigid, followed the latter but who, on learning that Saint Brigid had plucked her eyes out to destroy her beauty, repented, became a saint and built this church." A similar account was given by Sean Mhaguidhir with the addition that "the reason that Saint Brigid was called 'Brid Caoch' was because of her having blinded herself."[11]

Saint Mogue

The modern church of Kilnavart is dedicated to Saint Mogue or Moaedhog who was born quite near by, in about A.D. 555, on the island of Inisbreachmhaige (Breac-maig, i.e. The Wolf Plain), now called Port Island or St. Mogue's Island in Templeport Lake. He was descended from the race of Conn, Fighter of a Hundred, and was therefore a member of the Ui-Briuin race.

In his early days Saint Mogue travelled widely as a missionary in England and Wales and it is interesting to note that his name is perpetuated in the towns of Portmadoc and Tremadoc in Carnarvonshire. On his return to Ireland he founded the monastery of Ferns and became the first bishop of that diocese.

Saint Mogue's name is closely associated with the

Priory of Drumlane which is said to have been founded by St. Columcille, probably in the early part of the sixth century. Saint Mogue appears to have built another church on the site from which the earlier foundation had disappeared. It is said that while at Drumlane Saint Mogue had a wonderful vision in which he saw "all the ramifications of the family of Aedh Finn [the progenitor of the families of O'Rourke and O'Reilly] simultaneously, and their genealogical branches and ramifications of relationship, and further, the name of every great chief who should obtain sovereignty and authority to the end of the world."[12] In the vision Saint Mogue was commanded to raise "another honourable place in addition to Drumlane. . . and this will be one of the most lasting fires of entertainment; to wit, the fire of the place where Maedoc saw the vision, Drumlane; and Cuillin na bFer or Rossinver, Cell Mor Feidlimid (Kilmore)."

At Rossinver in the extreme northwest of the present Co. Leitrim St. Mogue erected "a strong and ample oratory and a fair built quadrangular regular church in preparation for his resurrection."[13] And here he died and was buried in the year 624, according to the Four Masters, though other authorities give the year 632.

During the reign of Pope John III (560–573), Saint Molaise of Devenish went on a pilgrimage to Rome and on his return to Ireland, bearing with him certain relics presented to him by the pope, he went to visit Saint Mogue and presented to him some of the relics which were said to include portions of the garments of the Blessed Virgin, and others pertaining to S.S. Peter and Paul. Apparently St. Mogue had a shrine or reliquary prepared in which to preserve these relics which was called the BREAC MOGUE. The origin of this curious term, Breac, meaning "speckled," is explained in the manuscript *Life of St. Molaise.*[14] Saint Mogue said to him "you have given me such a variety of objects that I am speckled with them."

Breac Moedóic (Breac Mogue), a reliquary or shrine, Saint Mogue had made to hold his sacred relics.

The Breac Mogue was preserved in Drumlane Abbey until the time of its confiscation, when the relic passed into the possession of the Mac Gaghran family and eventually into the possession of the parish priest of Drumlane. It appears that it was used as a sacred object on which to swear a binding oath and as such was borrowed and taken to various parts of the country; this gave rise to the saying "as true as if sworn on the Breac." However, from one of these borrowings, in 1840, it failed to return. The borrower sold it to a Dublin jeweller who in turn sold it to the distinguished antiquarian Dr. Petrie. On his death it passed to the National Museum where it now rests.

The shrine measures eight and seven eighths inches by three and a half; it is seven and a quarter inches high and is made of bronze. Canon O'Hanlon described it as follows:

It is formed like an ancient Cill or church. Its sides were covered with exquisitely formed figures of ecclesiastics habited in seventh or eighth century costumes. Besides the figures a great variety of ornamental designs executed in brown and variegated enamel may be seen. By competent critics this shrine has been pronounced to be the oldest, and the Irish workmanship the most interesting of its class known to remain in the world. In it are depicted Christ with the apostles Peter and Paul. The Redeemer holds in his right hand the book of the law and in his left a vase, closely resembling in form some old Irish chalices yet preserved in the Royal Irish Academy; while in the arcade or where he stands are birds, symbolic of the angelic choir. Saint Paul is at the right hand of Christ with a sword in the right and a sceptre in the left hand. Saint Peter stands at the left of Christ—this in many ancient memorials being the post of highest honour, with a sceptre in the right and a crozier in the left hand.[15]

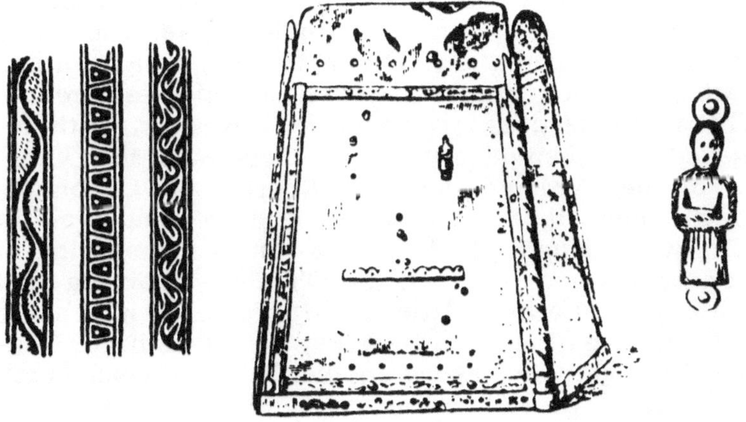

The Shrine of the Bell of Saint Moaedhog, said to have been presented to the infant Saint Mogue at the time of his baptism.

Another relic is the Clog Mogue or Shrine of Saint Mogue's Bell. It is said by tradition to have been presented to the infant Mogue at his baptism by Saint Caillin of Fenagh. This shrine was for centuries in the possession of the Magauran family, its hereditary custodians. On the death of the last of this family in 1833 his son-in-law sold it to the Reverend Marcus Beresford who later presented it to the Library of Armagh where it still remains.[16]

There is a legend that on the Last Day the people of Breifne would be judged by Saint Mogue:

> Over the men of Breifne, as is right,
> To save them from the wrath of the Creator,
> In Drumlane, on his own sacred soil,
> Gentle Maedoc is judge.

—O'Clery

The Priory of Drumlane

The ruins of St. Mary's priory of Drumlane lie about four miles south of the present town of Belturbet against the beautiful background of Drumlane lake. The abbey stood on a broad ridge (Druim Leatan), which formed part of the boundary between East and West Breifne. That was indeed its misfortune for it was constantly involved in the sanguinary encounters between the O'Reillys on the one hand and the O'Rourkes and O'Connors on the other. It was burned down in 1246 and again in 1261 when Hugh O'Connor the son of Felimy king of Connacht was defeated by the O'Reillys. Again, in 1314 there was another battle of Drumlane in which the O'Reillys were defeated by Rory, son of Cathal O'Connor. In 1338 there was yet another battle in which Hugh son of Rory was slain.

All that now survives of this venerable foundaton

Two views of the Drumlane Abbey ruins. Built in the 13th Century, it was the scene of many battles between the O'Reillys and the sons of Rory O'Connor.

are the abbey church, a round tower, and a fragment of the abbey wall. The church though roofless is in fair state of preservation; the tower, or what remains of it is about forty-five feet high, with an entrance about nine feet from the ground.

On the eastern face of the tower about six feet above the base there is a weather worn "Cock and Hen" carving. This is said to be based on the "Cock and Pot" legend concerning Judas Iscariot. The story goes that Judas returning home found his wife cooking a chicken. She upbraided him because of his act of betrayal and declared her belief in the Resurrection. Judas in a rage declared that the Resurrection was as likely as that the bird she was cooking should come to life, whereupon the bird flew out of the pot, flapped its wings and crowed thrice. O'Connell says that this legend is of great antiquity;[17] it is recorded in the *Leabhar Breac,* one of the earliest Gaelic manuscripts, and representations in sculpture are to be found on monumental slabs in many parts of Ireland, notably of the MacCreagh altar tomb dated 1537 at Lismore, County Waterford and on the Purcell monument dated 1549 in St. Canice's Cathedral, Kilkenny.

Tomregan

Not far away, to the northwest of Drumlane there once existed the great lay university of Tomregan (Tuaim Drecuin, i.e. The burial mound of Drecon). Here, in the seventh century there flourished a town which was the seat of a famous university; it had three schools, of Latin, Irish Law, Irish Learning. Of this great institution not a trace now remains.

> Where the quiet coloured end of evening smiles,
> Miles and Miles,
> On the Solitary pastures where the sheep

A "Cock and Pot" sculpture from tombstone on Rock of Cashel. "Cock and Pot" sculptures are based on an old legend about Judas Iscariot.

Half asleep,
Tinkle homeward thro the twilight, stay or stop
As they crop.
Was the site once of a city great and gay
(so they say) . . .
And such plenty and perfection, see, of grass
Never was!
Such a carpet as, this summertime, o'er spreads
And embeds.
Every vestige of the city, guessed alone,
Stock or stone—
Where a multitude of men breathed joy and woe
Long ago.

—Robert Browning

There is a fascinating story connected with the university of Tuaim Drecuin. Cenn Faelad, afterwards called Sapiens who was the Son of Aillil, was seriously wounded in the battle of Moira (Magh Rath) in 638 A.D. between the King of Ireland and his namesake, Domnall Brecc, King of Dalriada. Cenn Faelad who was aged about twenty-four, was fighting on the side of the High King; his skull was cleft in the battle. He was taken to Tuaim Drecuin "and brought to be cured at the house of Briccíne, at the meeting of the three streets between the houses of the three chief professors."[18] This Briccíne was a teacher as well as a practising surgeon. Cenn Faelad recovered from his wound after surgical treatment by Bricínne and his later achievements caused it to be told of him that "his brain of forgetting was taken from his head." Trepanning was of course a frequent practice in pre-historic Western Europe but the foregoing description suggests that this operation was something more than trepanning; it was really a form of lobotomy.

According to the Irish law of the period a person suffering from such an injury as Cenn Faelad's had to

44

remain under the surgeon's care for a period of three years. During that time Cenn Faelad attended the various departments of the university where he took copious notes and eventually became a distinguished historian, a poet, and an authority on the Brehon law; amongst other things he compiled a grammar of the Irish language. As professor MacNeill points out in the article from which this extract is taken, he was truly "a Pioneer of Nations." Briccíne was afterwards honoured as a saint by popular acclaim and his name is perpetuated in the townland of Slievebricin (Sliab Bricin, i.e Bricin's Hill) west of Mullynagolman two miles south of Ballyconnell.

Holy Trinity Priory

On Trinity Island in Loch Uachtair there are the remains of what was once a large and important religious foundation. In the year 1237 A.D., according to the *Annals of the Four Masters*, a monastery for Canons of the Premonstratensian order was commenced here by Clarus MacMaillin on a site granted by Cathal O'Reilly who was Chief of Breifne at the time. The subsequent development and ultimate fate of the Priory is closely bound up with that of the O'Reilly family and more will be said about this later.

The island on which the Priory was built was one of the largest in Loch Uachtair, comprising some 120 acres; there are in addition three other fairly large islands in the lake; Inch, Eonish (Eo Inis, i.e. the Yew Island), and Derinish (the Island of the Oaks).

O'Connell, writing in 1937, gives the following description of the ruins:

Approaching Trinity Island by boat from the direction of Bleancup or Killyvally the ivy mantled gable of the ruined church is a prominent feature of the landscape; this is the west gable which is still remarkably perfect and displaying a pointed window over a deformed and mutilated doorway. With the exception of this gable only fragmentary portions of the church remain.[19]

From measurements of the foundation walls O'Connell states that the church was 76 feet in length by 20 feet in width; there was also evidence of a side chapel on the south wall measuring 20 feet from north to south and 18½ feet from east to west. Scattered about the graveyard surrounding the church were fragments of slabs, some of them elaborately carved; local tradition says that a great deal of material was taken away from time to time for building purposes on the mainland. The head of a large crucifix was discovered close to the ruins in 1921;[20] the cross was eighteen inches high and beautifully carved front and back, it was of Celtic design and the circle was perfect, as also was the figure. The left arm was intact but the right arm and the top were broken off. It is of interest to note that in 1644 Monsignor Massari, secretary to the Nuncio, Archbishop Rinuccini, visited the priory ruins. "I found," he says "in a corner many painted and gilt images of saints carved in wood; they were lying exposed to wind and rain having been overturned by the heretics who dominated the district. If I remember aright, there was a crucifix, with statues of the Blessed Virgin and Child, of Saint Patrick, Saint Mary Magdalen, and three other saints."[21] It may very well be that the crucifix here referred to was the one discovered by Dr. Comey in 1921.

The Origin of Kilmore Diocese

The patron saint of Kilmore, and its first bishop was Feidhlimidh (Felimy). For so important a figure in the history of Breifne we know singularly little about him.

The exact date of his birth is unknown but it is believed to have been some time shortly after 500 A.D. His father was Carvill or Carrill whose family ruled over Cairbre Gabhra, a territory which stretched from northeast Longford to Loch Uachtair. His mother was Dediva, granddaughter of Dubtach Ui Lugair chief poet of Ireland who was converted to Christianity by Saint Patrick. Saint Felimy left home in his early youth and "retired to a secluded spot" in the neighbourhood of Kilmore.

In the early part of the sixth century Saint Columba (Colum) founded a monastery at Slanore (Snamh Luthir, i.e. the Swimming Place of Luthir) on a hillside rising abruptly from the shore of Upper Loch Erne. All trace of this monastery has disappeared but the site is commemorated in the "Abbey Field," a circular area somewhat under an acre in extent. Evidence of its former importance was demonstrated over a century ago when a large number of elaborately carved stones were unearthed in this field. The founder of this monastery was the son of Eochaidh, a descendant of the High King Laoghaire. Columba died in 640 A.D.[22]

Saint Columba's friend the great Saint Columbkille was a frequent visitor to Slanore. At some date in these early years of the sixth century he founded a monastery at Tonymore. All trace of it has disappeared but it is said that the holy well of Saint Felimy near the old cathedral of Kilmore marks the site.

There is some doubt whether Tonymore or Slanore was the secluded spot to which Saint Felimy retired in his youth but at all events, shortly after his consecration as bishop he built his own "Great Church," Cill Mor, the old cathedral of the diocese, which still stands.

In the early seventeenth century the old cathedral passed into Protestant hands and was renovated as a place of worship, at which time the famous doorway of Trinity Priory was removed and incorporated in the renovated cathedral; later, on the erection of the present

Doorway of Kilmore Cathedral. This doorway was originally used in the twelfth century Trinity Priory on Trinity Island in Loch Uachtair.

Protestant cathedral of Kilmore it was again removed
and utilised as the vestry door of the new building.

This doorway is one of the most interesting speci-
mens of its class in Ireland. Canon O'Hanlon has left us
a description of it:[23]

Kilmore Cathedral, County Cavan, Ireland. Erected in 1858.

It has chevron mouldings with a magnificently rounded arch
over connecting moulded and receding jambs. The stones are
all finely carved in zig-zag and interlaced patterns and it contains the most interesting and beautiful details of Irish architecture the world has yet seen. The stones seem composed
of a reddish gritty substance, weather worn yet with the carv-
ings all very sharply defined; except where some damage at
the angles has been supplied with a plain coating of cement
executed with good taste and judgment. The upper arch is of
considerable height and the doorway is of sufficient width to
afford easy access to the vestry through a modern door.

The distinguished archaeologist Dr Harold G. Leask
has argued cogently that the doorway belongs to the
second phase of Irish Romanesque architecture and can

be dated to the years 1160 to 1170 A.D. Dr Leask points out that the Kilmore doorway is almost identical with that of the Nun's Church at Clonmacnoise, and he is convinced that both doorways were designed by the same craftsman.[24] It is significant that at the time when the famous church of Clonmacnoise was founded by Dervorgilla, her husband Ternan O'Rourke was the most powerful chief in Breifne and the protector of the diocese, then known as the diocese of Ui-Briuin.

This raises the problem of how the Holy Trinity Priory founded in 1237 came to have a doorway which must have been created nearly a century earlier; and there is the related problem as to the apparent non-existence of a diocese of Kilmore during the twelfth century despite the fact that it is on record that the names of three bishops of the Ui-Briuin diocese during that period are known and it is also on record that one of them, Tuathal O Connachtaig, was present at the opening ceremony and session of the Synod of Kells in 1125. The probable answer to both problems has been set forth in a detailed article by Rev. Aubrey Gwynn. S.J. in the Breifne Journal for 1961. Briefly, it appears that in copies of early documents relating to the delineation of Irish dioceses the word Darinth or Darrich appeared and was wrongly interpreted by later writers as referring to the diocese of Derry, which however, did not come into existence until 1254.

Fr. Gwynn suggests that the word Darinth or Darrich is a corrupt rendering of Darinish, an island in Loch Uachtair and that this island was the site of an ancient monastery which at some early date became the cathedral church of the diocese of Dairinis, and that the doorway which can now be seen at Kilmore was formerly the chief ornament of the older cathedral church of Dairinis. Dr Gwynn continues, "We have become so accustomed to think of Kilmore as the cathedral of the diocese which

Seal of the Kilmore Diocese, founded in the 14th Century.

still bears its name that it may seem strange to suggest that another church was, for perhaps a hundred years the cathedral church of the diocese. Kilmore is not expressly mentioned as a cathedral church in early documents of the 13th or 14th centuries; we do not know the exact date at which the church of Kilmore became the cathedral church of the diocese of Tir Briuin. That it was not the cathedral church of the diocese in 1152 seems to be certain since no name at all like Cill Mor is to be found in the official lists of Irish dioceses approved at the Synod of Rathbreasail in 1111 A.D. or of Kells in 1125."[25]

Saint Dymphna

Throughout Breifne there are numerous holy wells dedicated to Saint Patrick and Saint Brigid, but there is a little-known one, the only one in Breifne or indeed, in all Ireland dedicated to Saint Dymphna. Dymphna (Daphne or Davnet) was the daughter of the pagan king of Oriel during the late sixth or seventh century A.D. She became a convert to Christianity and, refusing to conform to the pagan religion, fled from her home with several companions and eventually reached Belgium where she lived in peace and security for some time. Eventually her father discovered her hiding place; he followed her there and when she refused to return home, in a fit of uncontrollable rage he killed her. Her relics are preserved in a silver reliquary in the church at Gheel, a town about twenty-five miles east of Antwerp.

In the townland of Corrawillin, about a mile south of the old parish church of Lavey (Leamaid, i.e. "a place abounding in elms") there are the ruins of a small oratory, locally known as Saint Daphne's oratory or station. It is said that it commemorates the place in a ravine enclosed with woods where Dymphna and her companions took refuge during their flight. The position of the oratory is in many respects unique. It was erected on a small rocky eminence on the bank of a stream which flows through the ravine and just overlooks a small cascade. The stream has its origin in a small lake in Lavey townland and the cascade is called Eas Damnait, that is the waterfall of Saint Dymphna. On the face of the rocky bank, close to the cascade and about four feet above the stream is a tablet depicting the king in the act of beheading his daughter. Up until recent times this

The tablet at Saint Dymphna's Well near the townland of Corrawillin, Cavan, Ireland. Shows Saint Dymphna being beheaded by her
father.

spot was the scene of a regular "pattern" or station at which large numbers of people gathered.

By reason of her association with Gheel, Saint Dymphna has been adopted as the patron saint of the insane, Gheel being one of the earliest places to deal with the insane in a humane manner by incorporating them into the local community; indeed it might be said that the whole life of this little town revolves round its mental hospital which has pioneered the building of houses specially designed to allow suitable families to take one or more patients into their care.

Notes

1. *Tripartite Life*. Rolls Edition. Vol. I. p 93.
2. *Book of Armagh*. Edited by Revd. John Gwynne. D.D.
3. *Tripartite Life*.
4. *Book of Armagh*.
5. *Annals of the Four Masters*.
6. Samuel Ferguson "Burial of King Cormac."
7. Kilmore p 75.
8. U.J.A. Series 3. Vol. II. 1939. Prof. O. Davies.
9. Kilmore. p110.
10. Bennett & Elton *History of Corn Milling*. 4 Vols. London. 1898.
11. Bealoides. 1. M.L.4.; 1933-4. Eamonn O'Tuathail.
12. Lives of the Irish Saints. Vol.I. 1922. Revd. Chas. Plummer.
13. Opus Cit.
14. *Silva Gadelica*. Published by O'Grady. In R.I.A.
15. *Lives of the Irish Saints*. Vol. VIII N134 Canon O'Hanlon.
16. R.I.A. Proc. Vol VIII. 1863.
17. O'Connell. *Kilmore*.
18. Studies. Vol. XI. 1922. pp 13-28 & 435-446. Prof Eoin MacNeill
19. *Kilmore*.
20. B.A.S. Vol. I. 1921. Very Revd. M. Comey. D.D.
21. Opus Cit.
22. *Lives of the Irish Saints*. Vol. III. p 134. O'Hanlon.
23. *Irish Churches & Monastic Buildings*. I. Early Phases and the Romanesque. Prof Leask. Dundalk. 1955.
24. "Origins of the Diocese of Kilmore." Breifne. Vol. I. No. 4. 1961.

THE RACE OF CONN (UI-BRIUIN LINE)

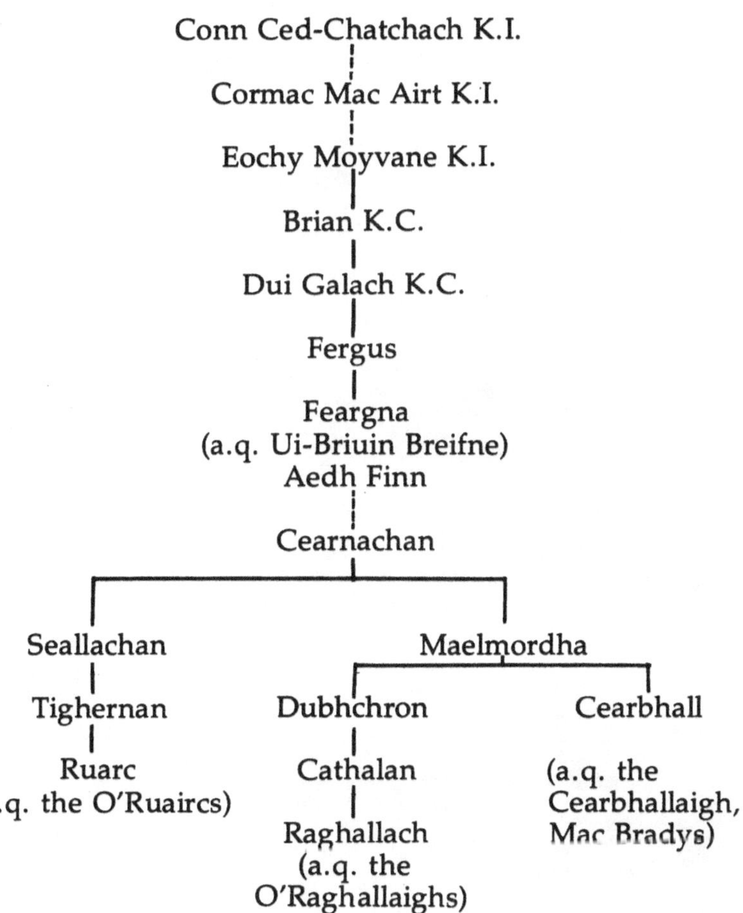

CHAPTER III

The Origin of the O'Reillys

> The Supreme leader of fierce encounters
> O'Reilly lord of bucklers red.
>
> —John Boyle O'Reilly

The O'Reillys, in common with a number of other Irish families, trace their origin to Conn Ced-catchach (Conn fighter of a hundred), High King of Ireland. One of his descendants was Brian King of Connacht in the fourth century A.D. and from him sprang the Ui-Briuin (the Race of Brian), including the Ui-Briuin Breifne "who swayed Breifne as kings and rulers from the sixth century down to the disastrous era of the Tudors when the structure of Gaelic dominion in Ireland—long previously battered and wrecked, and shaken to its foundations—finally crumbled to utter ruin."[1]

Brian was the son of Euchy Moyvane, King of Ireland from 357 to 365 A.D. (Incidentally he was the brother of Niall of the Nine Hostages.) He is reputed to have had 24 sons, and from one of these, Dui Galach, King of Connacht, came Fergus who died in 517 A.D. Feargna, the son of Fergus, was the immediate progenitor of the Ui-Briuin Breifne. Dui Galach who died in 463 A.D. is said to have been converted to Christianity by Saint Patrick. He was the common ancestor of the

O'Rourkes, O'Reillys, O'Connors, and O'Flahertys.

The transformation of the ancient territory of Breifne into Ui-Briuin Breifne dates from the northward migration of Feargna and his attendant retinue, and that migration may safely be referred to the middle of the sixth century.[2]

At that time the older inhabitants of Breifne were, notably, the Masraighe dwelling in the Magh Sleacht area and the Gailenga occupying the area round Loch Ramor. These groups were gradually subdued by the invaders until the Clann Ui-Briuin ruled supreme throughout Breifne.

On the death of Feargna his son Aedh Finn (Hugh the fair-haired) succeeded as ruler. He died in 611 A.D. In fulness of time two descendants of Aedh Finn appeared. These were Seallachan, the ancestor of the O'Ruaircs, and Maolmordha, the ancestor of the O'Raghallaighs. The O'Ruaircs became the ruling princes of West Breifne and the O'Raghallaighs, of East Breifne. In the oldest genealogical books the O'Reillys are called Muintir-Maolmordha (the people of Maolmordha or Milesius).

> Royal Lord of rough incursions
> Is O'Reilly of red weapons,
> The deliciousness of his golden voice
> Is heard over the polished Muintir Maolmordha

> —Topographical poem by O'Dugan

From Maolmordha through Dubhcron and Cathalan came Raghallach, the chieftain from whom the family name is derived; through another descendant of Maolmordha came Cearbhall from whom descended the Cearbhallaigh (the MacBradys). Raghallach is said to have been killed at the battle of Clontarf in 1014 A.D.

The name Raghallach is said to derive from "Ragh"

(Race) and "Ealach" (gregarious), but some authorities hold that the correct spelling is Radheolach, from "Radh" (a saying) and "Eolach" (skillful), in which case the correct spelling in Irish would be O'Radheollaigh.[3]

From Raghallach were descended, Airten, Airghiallach, Cu-Connacht, Mac na hOidche, and Godfraidh.

Godfraidh, fifth in descent from Raghallach and ruler of Breifne, was slain in a battle at Kells in 1161 A.D. by Melaghlin O'Rourke who also slew his son Giolla Iosa.[4] Another son of Gofraidh, Cathal na gCaorach (of the sheep), succeeded as ruler but he died in 1162 and was succeeded by his son Annadh who died in 1220.

All these men were styled King of Breifne but Annadh was the last to hold this title; henceforth they were styled Chief or Prince. Annadh left two sons, Cathal and Fergus or Fergal.

From the earliest times the O'Reilly chiefs were elected by their people and crowned on the summit of Shantemon (Sean Tuimin), a hill lying between the present towns of Cavan and Ballyhaise. The meaning of the word Shantemon is obscure; it may possibly be related to an ancient tumulus or burial mound associated with Druidic rites which undoubtedly took place there in earlier ages.

The Castle of Loch Uachtair

In the *Annals of Loch Cé* there is a reference under the year 1220 A.D. to an attack on "the Crannoge of O'Reilly" by De Lacy, Earl of Meath. At this time Cathal son of Annadh was Chief of Breifne and in 1224, taking advantage of the fact that De Lacy was at war with the king of Meath, with the help of Walter de Riddisford and Richard Tuite he recaptured it and also the Norman castle of Kilmore which he demolished, thus ending the effective domination of the Normans in East Breifne.[5]

The origin of Loch Uachtair Castle is shrouded in mystery. It is said to have been built on a crannoge in the lake at some early date. O'Donovan states "that it is a genuine crannoge, that is, partially or wholly of artificial formation in which timber was liberally used admits of no reasonable doubt."[6] As to the date of its erection he adds "Loch Uachtair was of note in 954 A.D.; the crannoge was there in 1220 and the castle was there in 1237. It is therefore at least 600 years old but it may be centuries older."[7] Petrie thinks it was built in the 11th century by one of the O'Reillys, while Orpen considers that it was built before 1220;[8] but the records speak of "O'Reillys Crannoge" at this time. This does not prove the existence of the castle as the island could have been occupied before the erection of a solid stone structure.

The first mention of the castle as such is in 1237[9] and the tradition of the O'Reilly pedigree is that it was built by Richard De Burgo, the Red Earl of Ulster in 1320 and was forcibly taken from him by the O'Reillys. The O'Reilly pedigree was composed about 1675 and so is not trustworthy for material more than a century earlier. It is doubtful if Richard De Burgo ever entered Breifne at all.[10]

Professor O. Davies is quite positive that the castle was built, not on a crannoge, but on a rocky crag which stands quite a short distance from the lake shore, in neighborhood of Killyvally, measuring 190 feet from north to south and 140 feet from East to West.[11] All that now remains of the castle is an empty shell; Professor Davies gives a detailed description of it. "The rafters of the first story are now [1946] about 20 feet from the lake level; in the 17th century the castle is described as rising directly out of the lake, which must have then been several feet higher. It is clear, as one would expect also, from the stability of the structure that the island is a rock and not, as has been frequently stated, artificial but along the flat sandy beach on the northeast are

Ruins of the Castle of Loch Uachtair, built on a crannoge in the lake sometime during the 13th Century.

traces of piles and beams, the remains of defensive out-works or quays.

"The ground floor was divided, apparently to the ceiling by a thick masonry wall. There is one recess or door in it. The floor of the first story rested on parallel joists running north to south and measuring 1ft. x 1ft. 3inches. The first storey, presumably containing the living rooms, seems to have been originally about 20 feet high, but at some time an intermediate floor was added. The second floor seems to be an insertion. On the northeast it has a rectangular window about 3ft. square.

"A good many objects have been found, mainly on the shore of the island. In the National Museum are a wedge-shaped stone, like an axe; a leaf-shaped sword of bronze; a socketed iron axe of Viking type; and a large copper coin."[12]

A number of references in the 14th century indicate the continued occupation of the castle,[13] but we do not hear of it in the 15th century because by this time the O'Reillys had moved their seat to the Castle of Tul-lymongan, so that Cloch Uachtair was then a refugee fortress of secondary importance. But there were many stirring incidents connected with it in succeeding cen-turies, as we shall see.

Tullymongan Castle

Just east of the present town of Cavan was the hill of Tullymongan (Tulach Mongain, i.e. Mongan's Hill). Who Mongan was or what connection he had with the hill is unknown. According to the O'Reilly pedigree[14] he was a Danish chief, Taoiseach Loclanach, who raised a fortress there; this seems highly improbable. It is much more likely that Mongan was an early Ui-Briuin chieftain who lived there long before the Danish invasion. In fact the name Mongan was well known in early times; it is recorded in the *Annals of the Four Masters* that in 624 A.D. Mongan Mac Fiaghra was killed by one Artur Ap Bicoir, a Welshman, with a stone. Mongan was the son of Fiaghra Lurgan King of Ulster or Ulidia as it was then known, for thirteen years; he died in 716 A.D. A similar account is given in the *Annals of Ulster* and in the *Annals of Clonmacnoise.*

The exact date of the erection of Tullymongan castle and the name of its builder are unknown; according to

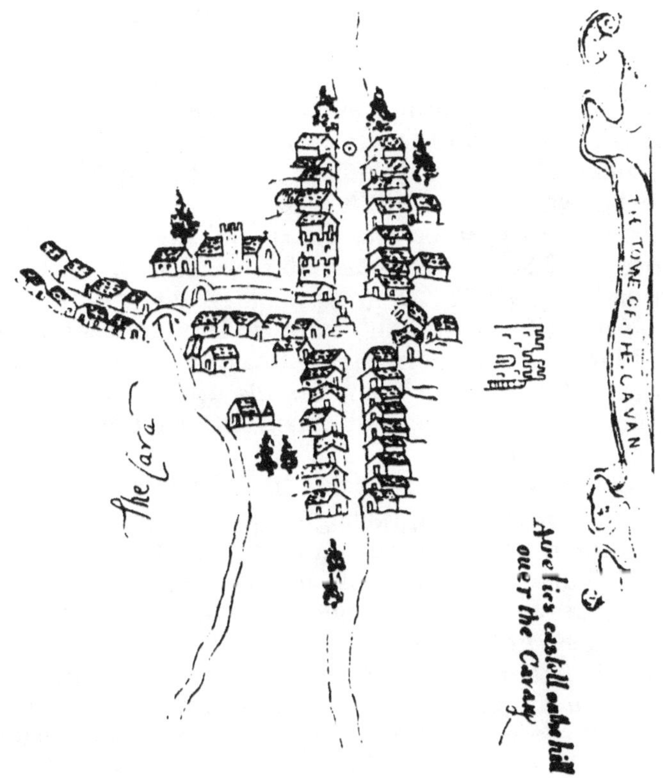

Circa 1593 map of Cavan Town, showing Castle Tullymongan, then known as Aurelies Castle.

the O'Reilly pedigree it was built by Toirdhealbach (Turlough) son of Sean an Einigh (the hospitable) about the year 1460 but the *Annals of the Four Masters* record the death of John son of Philip in the castle in 1400 and of Turlough, also in the castle, in 1487. A map of Cavan town dated 1593 shows "Auerelie's castell" on the hill over the Cavan (River). In the centre is depicted a market cross and a bullring.

The Founder of Holy Trinity Priory

According to the *Genealogical History of the O'Reillys* "Cathal son of Annadh was called Cathal na Beithighe and that he was so called from An Bheitheach where he lived, near Oiléan na Trinóide, or from An Bheitheach where he was slain, a little west of the Shannon."[15] It has been already noted that he demolished the castle of Kilmore in 1224. A few years later, in 1231, according to the *Annals of Loch Ce*, "a great hostage assembly was led by Domhnall O Domhnaill, king of Tirconaill, and Aenghus Mac Gillafhinnein against Cathal Ó'Raghallaigh; and they brought with them vessels upon Loch Uachtair and plundered Eo-Inis and killed the best white steed that was in Erin."[16]

It would appear that at this time Eo-Inis was the residence of Cathal O'Raghallaigh and, being very rich in jewels and other treasure, had aroused the cupidity of his neighbors. The reference to the white steed recalls the fact that the O'Reillys were famous throughout Ireland for their horsemanship.

In 1233 there was another invasion of Breifne, this time by the English. Again we read in the *Annals of Loch Cé* that "there was a hosting by William de Laici [son of Hugh and the daughter of Ruadhri son of Toirdhealbach Mor Ó Chonchobair], and by the foreigners of Midhe (Meath) along with him; when they went with great force into the Breifne to Cathal Ó'Raghallaigh and to his brother Cu-Connacht and committed great depredations. A party of the people of Ó'Raghallaigh, however, encountered William de Laici and the chieftains of the hosts who were behind the preys; and they gave each other battle, and William Brit was slain there, and other good foreigners along with him; and William de Laici was wounded there, and Charles son of Cathal Gall and many more along with them; and they [the foreigners] afterwards returned from the district without pledges or hostages; and William de Laici and Charles son of Cathal Gall Ó Conchobair, and Feorus Finn [Pierce the fair] son of the foreign Queen [Isabella, mother of Henry III] and Diarmaid Bernach Ó Maelsechlainn died in their own houses immediately after from the wounds inflicted on them at Móna-Crand-Chain."[17]

Móna-Crand-Chain (Mónai-Crand-Cain, i.e. "the bog or morass of the beautiful trees"), the site of the battle, was in the townland of Legnaderk beside Bellyvally Gap among the mountains of Tullyhaw.

In 1237 Cathal granted a site on Trinity Island in Loch Uachtair to the Pre-Monstratensian Canons for the establishment of a monastery and later, in 1250, granted the whole island to them in perpetuity. In the same year Cathal was involved in an unsuccessful expedition against the O'Neills of Tyrone.

In 1256 Cathal and his supporters went on a raid against Felim O'Connor king of Connacht. A fierce battle was fought at Magh Sleacht and Cathal was slain by Felim's son Hugh. The *Annals of Loch Cé* give details of those slain in the battle: "Cathal O'Raghallaigh king of Muintir Maolmordha and the descendants of Aedh Finn, together with his sons, viz. Domnhnall Ruadh and Niall, and his brother Cu-Connacht; and the three sons of Cathal Dubh O'Raghallaigh—The battle of Magh Sleacht on the brink of Ath-Derg, at Alt-na-Helti over Bealach-na-Beithighe is the name of this battle."[18] A similar account is given in the *Annals of the Four Masters* and in the *Annals of Ulster*.

Niall the son of Cathal who perished with him in this battle was nicknamed An Caoch (the blind one), because on one of his expeditions against the English he was captured and taken in fetters to Dublin. There he was given the choice of three things: the loss of progeny, the loss of feet, or the loss of eyes. He chose loss of eyes and, in accordance with the judgment, he himself plucked out his eyes; the name Caoch gradually replaced that of O'Reilly in this branch of the family, and the patrimony granted to him by Cathal was known as Clankee. His descendants took the name Caoch or in some cases, Mc Kee, until 1671 when the Primate Oliver Plunkett refused to allow the friar Sean, son of Cathal Dubh to be ordained unless he called himself O'Reilly instead of Caoch.

In the *Genealogical History of the O'Reillys*[19] there is a gruesome story related under the heading of Cathal-na-Beithighe and how the Sheridans came to Breifne.

After the battle of Magh Sleacht Cathal's head was taken to the residence of the king of Connacht and there hung under the droppings of the Royal candle. O'Siridean, a blind man, was in the town and one of his sons was cupbearer to O'Conor. He took pity on the head and, passing backwards and forwards he used to put the beginning and the end of every drink on the head. O'Conor was told that he was only drinking the leavings of a dead man, and on hearing this he sentenced the cupbearer to be put in a limekiln. However, the latter learnt of this in time to get away and the whole family hurriedly fled. In the course of their journey they came to the residence of Feargal an Tochar O'Reilly who was Chief of Breifne at the time. The O Ruaircs were then in possession of Loch Uachtair castle and Feargal promised them that if they could regain the castle he would give them the place and the land. The Sheridans along with several supporters lay in wait for the O Ruairc vassals and slew them when they came to the mainland to collect firewood. Dressing themselves in the victims' clothing they got across to the castle by boat and slew all within before they could put up any resistance. In this way, says the scribe "they got the best land in Breifne, that is from Loch Uachtair to Mullach Luch."

A verse appended to this tale shows that Cathal was a thoroughly unpopular individual:

> The king of the Ui Briuin of the bright standards,
> few people love him,
> O'Raghallaigh of Mag Sleacht
> who boasted of no deed done by his hand.

It may be added that there is a tradition that Cathal's body was conveyed from the battlefield to the Priory of Loch Uachtair for burial. Cathal's brother, Cu-Connacht who perished with him at Magh Sleacht must also have been a somewhat unsavoury character. In the *Annals of the Four Masters* under the year 1224 it is recorded that "Teige, son of Red Handed O Conor was deprived of his sight and hanged on the festival of Saint Berach by Cu-Connacht O Raghallaigh on Inis-na-Conaire [O'Reilly's Island] in Loch Allen, sometimes called Inisfayle, having been kept in confinement by him since St. Martin's Eve."[20]

Dohmnall Mor, son of Cathal, had three sons, Matha, Fearghal, and Giolla Iosa Ruadh. The following tale is told about Matha. "Matha was notably charitable. On that account, having given a cloak to a monk, he got a promise that he would not die without a priest. And they say that he had a long lingering disease, and that he said to the clergy of Druim Leathan who used to come often to visit him: 'It is a great shame to see the community of Druim Leathan going away empty-handed.' Later they neglected him and he died without a priest. They went with the body to Druim Leathan, and as they came to Lios Droma dha Mhanach they saw two monks, one attired to say Mass, and the other opening the bier, so that Matha arose, made his confession, and died afterwards."[21]

After the burial Giolla Iosa Ruadh recited:

> O man who places the heavy stone
> on the bright gentle body of Dohmnall's son,
> on Matha it were not fitting to put
> save satin and stones of crystal.

Matha, who was the O'Raghallaih on the death of Cathal na Beighighe, died in 1281 and was succeeded by his brother Fearghal who was himself slain by Nicol na Tuaithe Mac An Mhaighistir.[22]

These repeated sanguinary encounters were to a large extent dictated by the social and economic setup of these early times. The social unit was the family group called the *derbfine* which consisted of all those related to one another in the male line, up to second cousins.[23] A number of such family groups made up the *tuath* [tribe or petty kingdom] constituting a semi-independent unit: there were about a hundred tuatha in Ireland grouped in seven over-kingdoms which in turn came under the general sovereignty of Cashel in the south and Tara in the north.

Early Christian Ireland was a land of cattle, and its economy was, to a remarkable degree, pastoral. There was no currency, and the basic units of value and exchange were the cow and the *Cumal* [literally "bondswoman"] which was worth four cows. Wealth was reckoned not so much in acres of land as in head of cattle. Cattle raiding [preys], i.e. "armed forays by a king or chief with his followers into the territory of another, to drive off as much stock as they could round up," was so common a form of warfare that it must be regarded as no more than a violent and bloody sport, a test of manhood and aristocratic stock, as much taken for granted as fox hunting was, until recent times.

The Founder of Cavan Monastery

One of the most outstanding figures in the long line of the ruling chiefs of Breifne was Giolla Iosa surnamed Ruadh (The Red). The name means "Servant of Christ" and was a common Christian name amongst the early O'Reillys. According to the *Genealogical History* he was an illegitimate son of Domhnall Mór and a woman of the family of Mág Goillsionnán and served as a scullion in his father's house,[24] for had he been legitimate it is unlikely that there would have been so little care of him. When the cook was in a hurry to roast a joint he declared that he would reward whoever brought him a piece of fuel. Thereupon Giolla Íosa Ruadh tore off his black greased tunic and put it under the pot, and there was mocking laughter inside [the house]. An Bodhar Mág Goillsionnán said that that was a laugh at the makings of a prince. Whatever his origin he was generous and pious, for they say that it was he who built the Monastery of Cavan and that in the end he went there to repent. Furthermore, he was a soldier of doughty deeds, as is clear from the poetical composition made by Maolaire O Maoileagan:

> We went on a spoiling
> with Giolla Iosa, the valorous;
> we spoiled the fort of Cruachain,
> and from there to Innse an Chláir.   [Ennis County Clare]

> The spoil and captives of Connacht
> (that was valorous success)
> were taken by Dohmnall's son,
> though he regarded not hardship of mind.

> O Gabhann was destroyed there
> and Mac Giolla Dhuibh was slain;

> Mag Bradaigh was slain there,
> that was the overcoming of the white horse.
>
> The displaying of the standards of Maol
> Sheachlainn
> we burnt widely
> from Aughrim to white Burren.[24]

Giolla Iosa Ruadh became ruler of Breifne in 1293. In the year 1300 he granted a large plot in what is now the centre of Cavan town together with a considerable acreage of surrounding lands for the establishment of a monastery.

According to Archdall, "The monastery of the Virgin Mary was founded in the year 1300 by Giolla Íosa Ruadh O'Reilly dynast of Breifne for friars of the Order of Saint Dominick; but the same sept of the O'Reillys, about the year 1393, expelled the Dominicans and gave the House to the conventual Franciscans."[25] On the other hand the O'Reilly Pedigree states that "The monastery of Cavan was founded by Giolla Íosa Ruadh, anno 1300, for the friars of Saint Francis";[26] and the overwhelming weight of evidence supports this version.

As we shall see the monastery suffered many vicissitudes throughout the centuries of its existence, and to-day all that remains of it is the ivy covered tower standing at a neglected street corner surrounded by weeds and debris; recently it has suffered the final indignity of being used as a fixing point for an electricity cable.

Giolla Iosa Ruadh was a man of considerable power and influence, not merely in Breifne, but throughout Ireland and abroad. Before he died he had made Breifne pretty well impregnable against the English. In 1314 Edward II of England addressed a letter to "Gillys O Raghli Duci Hibernorum de Brefny" asking for the support of the Irish chieftain in his enterprises.

According to the *Annals of Loch Cé* under the year 1330: B.C.

Tower of Franciscan Monastery, Cavan, Ireland. Founded by Giolla
Íosa Ruadh in 1300.

Giolla Íosa O Raghallaigh, King of Muintir Maolmordha
and all the Breifne for a long time previously, died a prosperous and wealthy senior, after obtaining victory over the devil
and the world. He was buried in the Franciscan Monastery in
Cavan.[27]

Giolla Íosa Ruadh is said to have had thirteen sons.
One of them, Maol Sheachlainn, seems to have been as
doughty a warrior as himself. He was a thorn in the side
of the English, so much so that they put pressure on
Giolla Íosa to hold him in check. Maol Sheachlainn's re-
ply to this was to attack the camp of the Lord Deputy,
whom he slew, carrying off his head. The *Genealogical
History of the O'Reillys* contains a poem by Giolla Íosa on
the exploits of his son:

> —The plunderer of the expanse of Midhe
> the gatherer, the spender,
> the man who has great generosity with the
>   Englishman's cattle,
> Maol Sheachlainn O Raghallaigh.

> The place where he set his house
> looks over Eamhain and Uisneach,
> out over the expanse of Midhe
> and the floor of the House of Tara.

For he lived at the top of Mullach, which is one of
the great heights of the country. They say that he had
tribute of a barrel of wheat and a barrel of malt from every ploughland from the gate of Ceananas (Kells) to the
gate of Baile Átha Cliath (Dublin).

Maol Sheachlainn had four sons, Fergal, Richard the
Bishop, Henry, and Gofraidh. Richard was bishop of
Kilmore from 1356 to 1369. In the *Annals of Loch Cé* he is
referred to as "Bishop of the Breifne." He appears to
have been a rather turbulent individual who had some

difficulty in accepting Church discipline. He was frequently in trouble with the Primate, Sweteman, of Armagh and was in fact excommunicated by him in 1366. However, after lengthy negotiations in which Philip O'Reilly, Chieftain of Breifne was involved, he swore to abide by the commands of the Church and was duly absolved and reinstated in his episcopal jurisdiction. His death is recorded in the *Annals of Loch Cé* in the year 1369: "Richard O'Reilly, Bishop of the Breifne in Christi quievit."

The charitable explanation of his stormy behaviour would seem to be that he suffered from some form of mental instability which rendered him, at times, not responsible for his actions. He was succeeded by John O'Reilly, son of Gofraidh. It seems that he also was a stormy petrel; in 1389, because of his inability or unwillingness to cooperate with the higher ecclesiastical authorities, he was deposed, though he appears to have become reconciled and restored to the episcopate shortly before his death in 1393.

Another of Giolla Íosa's sons was Mathghamhain (Mahon), ancestor of the lords and nobles of Clanmahon. "They were so strong against the English that every stronghold almost, that they used to make during the day was levelled during the night. In a single day Tomás son of Mathghamhain levelled eighteen castles that the Tuites had built, and not a single one of these castles was raised since. It is he, too, who built Caisleán an Lacha, and all that lay between the town of Athlone and Drogheda was under tribute and "cutting" to him.[28]

Caisleán an Lacha was Crover Castle which Tomas built in the late 14th century, on a small islet near the eastern shore of Loch Sheelin. The castle, or what is left of it, stands about ten feet above the level of the lake. It figured in a tragic romance which we shall consider in detail later.

Giolla Íosa Ruadh was succeeded as ruler of Breifne

by his son Cu-Connacht. There was apparently some enmity between Cu-Connacht and his brother Philip for he kept him for some time a prisoner in chains, in Cloch Uachtair. Concerning this incident there is a curious story in the *Genealogical History*. "They say that Seaán, son of Philip, son of Giolla Íosa Ruadh, had another family, and that he had two wives, the daughter of Ó'Ruairc and the daughter of Ó Néill. This was the position of Philip; he was in fetters in Cloch Uachtair—Then his son Seaán sought help from Ó Ruairc his father-in-law. Ó Ruairc made excuses. Ó Ruairc's daughter saw the plight in which Philip was: he had no allowance save a sheaf of oats for day and night, and a cup of water, so that he was compelled to drink his own urine. And she said to Seaán: 'Since you did not get help from my father leave me and take another wife with whom help will be got. And when there is peace let you have the wife you wish, or the wife who has most right to you.'

"He accepted the advice and took to wife the daughter of Ó Néill. She apparently bore him four sons and it is after her is named 'the line of Ó Néill's daughter,' that is, the offspring of Conchobar, son of Fearadach, in Clanmahon. However, when she died, or when he left her, he took back his own wife.

"O'Neill sent a great host with Sean so that he defeated Cu-Connacht, released his father and he [i.e.Philip] was made Chief."[29] Whether as a result of this defeat or from the prickings of a guilty conscience, Cu-Connacht in 1365 resigned the chieftancy to his brother Philip and retired to the Franciscan monastery where he died two years later.

There is a seal matrix in the Victoria & Albert Museum, London which belonged to Cu-Connacht. It is of silver and measures one inch in diameter. Unfortunately the centre piece is missing, the legend alone remaining. This is in Lombardic capitals and appears to read:

Two views of the Seal of Cu-Connacht O'Reilly, son of Giolla Iosa Ruadh, 14th Century chief of Breifne.

✚ S.CONCONhAChT ORA GILLICI

Dr. Philip O'Connell has pointed out[30] that when rearranged in separate gaelic words the legend reads "S. CON CONNACHT O Raghallaigh," which may be translated "The Seal of Cu-Connacht O Raghallaigh." He adds that although there were other O'Reilly chieftains of the same name, the son of Giolla Íosa Ruadh was the most prominent of them and we may conclude that this was his seal.

Philip O'Reilly became chieftain in 1365 but four years later, in 1369 he was deposed and imprisioned in Loch Uachtair castle. His supporters gathered an army and, aided by the MacMahons of Oriel, they marched to Cloch Uachtair to release him. The usurping chief, Manus O'Raghallaigh marched against them, drawing up his forces across Bleancup Hill between two lakes to intercept the invaders; he was completely defeated, Philip was released and restored to the chieftaincy. In the following year Manus in his turn, was imprisioned in the castle.

Philip died in 1384 and was succeeded by Tomas, son of Mathgamhain, who died in 1390. John, son of Philip, then succeeded to the chieftaincy. According to the *Annals of Ulster* he died in 1401 "of a fit, in his own bed in Tulach Mongain and was buried the same night in Cavan."

John was succeeded by Maolmordha, son of Cu-Connacht. He died in 1411 and was succeeded by Richard Óge, Lord of Clanmahon and Breifne. He was the son of Richard Mór, son of Tomas. Unfortunately he was drowned only six years later in Loch Sheelin. Along with him perished his son Eóghan and Philip O'Reilly, Dean of Drumlane. The only survivor was Richard's wife, Finnguala, daughter of Mag Raghnall who was evidently a powerful swimmer and managed to gain the shore. Richard was succeeded in the barony by his son Ruaidhrig (Rory).

The next ruler of Breifne was Eóghan, son of John, son of Philip. He was known as Eóghan na Féasóige (the Bearded). In the year 1429, taking advantage of a quarrel between the O'Rourkes and the O'Reillys, the English made an attack on the town of Cavan, plundered and burnt it. Eoghan called on the O'Neills for aid, and together with the chieftains of Oriel, and Fermanagh, they marched against the armies of the Pale. They inflicted a terrible defeat on the English at the battle of Achadh-Cille- Moire ("the field of the big wood"). The *Annals of Ulster* record the death of Eóghan in 1449:[31]

Eóghan son of John Ua Raghallaigh, namely King of the two Breifne, died this year, about the feast of Saint Patrick; to wit, a man that completely defended his territories against their neighbours. He died with victory of penance and was buried in the Monastery of Cavan.

The *Annals of Breifne* tell us that "it is this Eóghan who, with lay and ecclesiastical consent, composed the statutes by which the men of Breifne abide."

Eóghan na Féasóige was succeeded by his son Séan an Einigh (John the Hospitable). During his reign in 1452, a catastrophe occurred at the monastery which was burnt to the ground. It was due to the carelessness of one of the friars named Ua Mothlain. According to the *Annals of Ulster:*

The candle he took with him to his chamber was left lighting and he himself fell asleep and the chamber took fire and the whole monastery afterwards, he being enebriated with wine."

The *Annals of Breifne* take a kindlier view of the incident, suggesting that the accident occurred while he was saying his office at night by candle.

Before his death in 1460 John had the monastery repaired and rebuilt. In that year he was killed fighting aginst the English. Along with him perished his brother and Eoghan, son of Mathgamhain MacCabe, Constable of Cavan.

The MacCabes were the Constables, that is the leaders of the gallowglasses of Breifne. They came from the Scottish Hebrides which in Irish were called the "Innse Gall" or Isles of the Norsemen. The name gallowglass (galloglach) means Norse or foreign soldiery. The population of the Hebrides was of mixed Norse and Gallic race, and they followed the wandering and fighting traditions of their Viking ancestors. In 1258 Donal Oge O'Donnell arrived in Ireland bringing with him a band of these Scottish gallowglasses. This was their first appearance in Ireland but within a short period they had penetrated to every part of the country and every Gaelic chieftain of any standing had to have his band of gallowglasses. Amongst those who migrated to Ireland about the year 1350 were the Mc Cabes who became the O'Reilly gallowglasses. They were stalwart mercenary soldiers who were much better equipped to withstand the heavily armed Normans than the native Irish in their light linen tunics:

> Unequal they came to the battle,
> The Foreigners and the race of Tara;
> Fine linen shirts on the race of Conn,
> The Foreigners one mass of iron.

The gallowglasses made an enormous difference to the efficiency of the native forces against the invaders, "tall, fierce, clad in helmet and coat of mail, and wielding battle axes as tall as themselves." Ultimately the Mc Cabes became a recognized Breifne sept, their chieftain being "The Constable of the Two Breifnes." The battle axe is prominent on their coat of arms and their motto was *Aut Vincere Aut Mori*. At the military funeral accorded to Henry Mc Cabe it was said that more than 280 battle axes were carried.

Notes

1. B.A.S.Jn. Vol. III, No. 1. 1927. John P. Dalton.
2. Op. cit.
3. *O'Hart's Irish Pedigrees*, 3rd Edition. 1881.
4. *Duffy—The O'Reillys at Home & Abroad.* John O'Donovan.
5. U.J.A. 1946-48. Vols. 10-12. Series III. Castles of Cavan. Prof. O. Davies.
6. Duffy. Vol. II. Jan-May. 1861.
7. op. cit.
8. *Ireland under the Normans.* Vol.III.p33. Orpen.
9. A.F.M.
10. Gen. Hist.
11. U.J.A. 1946-48. Vols. 10-12. Series III. Castles of Cavan.

12. Op. cit.
13. *Annals of Loch Cé, 1369. & A.F.M. 1369-70.*
14. M.S.H. (15 T.C.D.)
15. Gen. Hist. p116. (48).
16. *Annals of Loch Cé. Vol.I. p415.*
17. *Annals of Loch Cé.*
18. *Annals of Loch Cé.*
19. Gen. Hist. p 116.(48).
20. *Annals of the Four Masters*
21. Gen. Hist. p 114.(45).
22. Op. cit. p 114.(46).
23. *Early Christian Ireland.* de Paor.
24. *Gen Hist.* p 115. (47).
25. *Monesticon Hibernicum,* p 40. Archdall.
26. *Book of Genealogies.* R.I.A. Ms. 26.D17.
27. *Annals of Loch Ce*
28. Gen Hist. p 106. (37).
29. Op. cit. p 105.(36).
30. *Kilmore.*

CHAPTER IV

The Calm Before the Storm

> Now is the winter of our discontent
> Made glorious by this son of York

> —Shakespeare, *Richard III*

By the year 1400 there had been a considerable rapprochment between the native Irish and the descendants of the original Anglo-Norman invaders, so much so that these latter had adopted the language and customs of the Irish and had intermarried freely with the old Gaelic aristocracy; Richard, brother of the fourth or "white Earl" of Ormond, married a Catherine O'Reilly and founded a family which ultimately succeeded to the Earldom. In 1480 Eleanor sister of Garett Mór Earl of Kildare married Conn the eldest son of the O'Neill.

But long before this, William De Burgo, founder of one of the most powerful Anglo-Norman families, who came to Ireland with Prince John in 1185, married, in 1193, the daughter of Donal Mór O'Brien King of Thomond. The De Burgos eventually became Earls of Ulster; in 1333 William De Burgo "The Brown Earl" was murdered by some of his tenants. His widow fled to England with her only child, Elizabeth. This Elizabeth married Lionel Duke of Clarence, Edward III's son. They had a child, Phillipa, who married Edmund Mortimer

Earl of March. Roger Mortimer, son of Edmund had a daughter Anne, who married Richard Duke of Cambridge, another son of Edward III: their son was Richard Duke of York, father of Edward IV. Thus did the blood of Brian Boru flow down through the Mortimers to the present Royal House of England.[1]

These descendants of the Normans, now stigmatised by the English colony of the Pale as "degenerate English" began to model themselves on the Gaelic chieftains and in defiance of the Monarchy acquired large areas of the country which they ruled over, just like the Gaelic kings. Gradually they built up, in the Irish Parliament, what came to be called the Patriot Party, with the avowed intention of achieving a degree of legislative independence for the Parliament and Government of Ireland.

This aspiration received a considerable impetus with the arrival in Ireland in 1447, of Richard Duke of York as Lord Lieutenant. To the Anglo-Irish he stood for the great names of De Burgo, Lacy, and Mortimer, his ancestors; to the Irish he was "Lord of the English in Ireland" in whose veins flowed the blood of Brian Boru. The Irish chieftains flocked in to do him homage, and prominent amongst them were the MacMahons and the O'Reillys.

In February 1460 Richard summoned a parliament at Drogheda, and here the Patriot Party put forward an unequivocal declaration that "The land of Ireland is and at all times hath been corporate of itself by the ancient laws and customs used in the same, free of the burden of any special law of the realm of England, save only such laws as by the lords spiritual and temporal and the commons of the said land have been in Great Council or Parliament there held, admitted, accepted, affirmed, and proclaimed."

As a possible aspirant to the English Crown this was not a proposition that commended itself greatly to

Richard, but since his main purpose was to get the people of Ireland on his side in the coming struggle with the Lancastrians he accepted it, with his tongue in his cheek. Truly it might be said that "the good old Duke of York" not only "marched them up the hill," he "led them up the garden path" as well.

Needless to say these developments caused considerable alarm in England, and as soon as Edward IV was firmly seated on the throne he determined to crush the Home Rule aristocracy. He sent over as his Lord Lieutenant, Sir John Tiptoft, Earl of Worcester, whose brutal crusade against the enemies of the House of York had earned him the title of "The Butcher." Amongst other foul deeds he seized the Earl of Desmond and beheaded him, a judicial murder which raised cries of horror, not only in Ireland but throughout England as well.

In 1468 Tiptoft invaded Cavan, and both the monastery and the castle of Tullymongain were burnt to the ground. It is salutary to recall that in 1470 during the temporary eclipse of Edward IV Tiptoft was captured by the Lancastrians and given a dose of his own medicine; they beheaded him.

In this same year died Cathal who had succeeded his brother John as "The O'Reilly." He in turn was succeeded by his nephew Turlough (Terence) who at once set about re-building the castle and the monastery. During his reign another O'Reilly presided over the diocese of Kilmore. He was John O'Reilly O.S.A., formerly Abbott of Kells County Meath; he was consecrated bishop in 1467. The exact date of his death is not known but it was probably in 1475 or 6. During Bishop O'Reilly's episcopate, Breifne suffered much from war and invasion and his task was a difficult one. He was a wise and energetic bishop, who laboured incessantly to mitigate the abuses which followed in the train of the English invasions.

After a reign of 20 years Turlough died on September 1, 1487. The *Annals of the Four Masters* record that he "died of a fit in his own castle of Tullymongain." He was buried with full honours in the Monastery of Cavan.

John, his son, succeeded him but only reigned for a brief period. The *Annals of Ulster* record his death under the year 1491:[2]

Ua Raghallaigh, namely John son of Toirdhealbach, son of John Ua Raghallaigh, to wit, a distinguished youth died this year in the beginning of his felicity [i.e. in the beginning of his reign] and was buried in the Monastery of Cavan, the 25th day of November, namely the feast of St. Catherine.

At this time the plague was raging throughout Ireland and in all probability this was the cause of John's early demise.

Another John, grandson of Eóghan na Féasoige now succeeded. At first he was opposed by Turlough's son Cathal who took possession of the castle of Tullymongain, but he was carried off by glandular fever in 1497, according to the *Annals of Ulster.*

Like many of his predecessors John was frequently involved in repelling invasions by the English of the Pale; and in this he was highly successful, but in 1495 there occurred another of those internecine quarrels which caused so much unnecessary havoc amongst the Irish clans. A battle took place in which John's son Turlough was slain by Cu-Connacht grandson of Maol-mordha of the Mullagh. John himself survived the encounter and a fortnight later, re-took the castle of Tullymongain which had been occupied by Cathal.

Another event which took place in John's reign was a change in the occupation of Cavan monastery. The *Annals of Ulster* under the year 1502 tell us that "the monastery of Cavan was negotiated from this year by Ó'Raghallaigh, namely John son of Cathal to the Friars of [strict] Observance against the Friars of the Common Life [i.e. the Conventuals]."

John O'Reilly died in 1510 leaving three sons, Fergal, Cahir, and Maolmordha. He was succeeded by his brother Aodh. Once again, in 1514, there was a major invasion of Breifne by the English under Gerald, Earl of Kildare. The castle of Tullymongain was captured and wrecked, Aodh, his brother Philip, and Philip's son were slain, together with several of the O'Reilly chieftains; the Constable of Breifne, Maine Mc Cabe, one of Tullymongain's stoutest defenders, was captured.

Cathal, the son of Eoghan na Féasóige had five sons of whom three, Seaan, Aodh, and Eóghan, ruled Breifne in turn, the latter succeeding on the death of Aodh. Eóghan Ruadh as he was known built the castle of Tullyvin. The barony of Tullyvin was one of the most important in Breifne in the late 16th century. The castle stood on an isolated rocky boss just above the river Annalee with an artificial fosse on the west side. In 1567 it was granted to Edmond O'Reilly "for the use of the Queen." All trace of it has long since disappeared.

Eóghan died in 1526, "one for whom All Ireland, both clergy and laity was full of esteem, for the excellence of his nobleness and his generosity, died with the victory of unction and penance."[3] He was succeeded by his nephew, Fergal, who was a great grandson of Eóghan na Feasoige. He reigned until 1535; he had four sons, Turlough, Aodh, Brian an Duthair and Eoghan Buidhe.

There is a story in the Genealogical History concerning Brian. It appears that his brother Turlough incited him to murder Tomas O Raghallaigh, the aged lord of Clanmahon and when his father, Fergal, learned of this act of treachery he put a curse on his family and he besought God that none of them should become Lord or Tanist (heir), nor that they should have progeny; and that he should not survive long with them. "On that account no son was born to them for eighteen years until Brian an Chogaidh was born, who was without hair or beard while he lived." Furthermore Fergal enjoined his brother Maolmordha that he should take the lordship after his own death. Fergal died before a year had passed, as he had asked, and was succeeded by Maolmordha despite some initial opposition by his nephew Turlough. Maolmordha's reign proved to be the most momentous in the long history of Breifne.[4]

Notes

1. *A History of Ireland*. Curtis.
2. *Annals of Ulster*.
3. Gen. Hist. p 79. (5).

CHAPTER V

The Decline of O'Reilly Power

> . . . . now bound in with shame,
> With inky blots, and rotten parchment bonds.
>
> —John of Gaunt, in Shakespeare's *Richard III*

Following Henry VIII's breach with the Pope the need was felt to bolster up his claim to be the Head of the Church in Ireland as well as in England, and also to gain the support of the Anglo-Irish aristocracy; and indeed, of the Gaelic chieftains if possible. But with the cunning which characterised that astute monarch Henry chose an approach quite different from that of his predecessors. He eschewed entirely any idea of conquest or plantation and adopted a policy of "sober ways, politic drifts, and amiable persuasion." Needless to say this policy was not adopted for any humane reasons but solely because it was estimated that the armed forces at the disposal of the Irish chiefs were so great, some 22,000, that any attempt at forcible conquest would be too risky a procedure.

The method by which this "amiable persuasion" was to be achieved was by the policy of "surrender and re-grant." Under this scheme the Gaelic chiefs who held their lands by Irish law, and those Anglo-Normans who could not prove title under English law, were to surrender their titles to the Crown and receive them back as "estates-in-tail" from the Crown. "The Irish lords," said Henry, "may be told that though we are above the law we will take nothing that belongs to them."

Under this arrangement many of the most prominent chiefs agreed to accept Henry as head of the Church and to renounce the ecclesiastical authority of the Pope. The O'Neill, in the person of Conn Bacach, regarded by many as the uncrowned king of Ireland, in December 1541, accepted Henry as King and Head of the Church, and promised to hold his lands by knight service, and to attend Parliament and answer the summons of the Deputy with a stated number of armed men; in return he was offered and accepted the title of Earl of Tyrone. The same terms were offered to The O'Donnell and to Murrough O'Brien who was created Earl of Thomond and Baron of Inchiquin.[1]

At this time Maolmordha was The O Raghallaigh. He was married to Margaret, daughter of Hugh Dubh O'Donnell chief of Tir Conaill. They had six sons, Aodh Conallach (Hugh of Tir Conaill), Edmund of Kilnacrott (Coill na Cruite, i.e. "the wood of the small hills"), Cahir, Eoghan, Thomas, and Philip the Prior (An Prioir Mór); the latter married the daughter of Christopher, son of the Baron of Delvin.

It was proposed to incorporate Breifne into the English system and to convert Maolmordha into a peer of the English type with the title of Viscount Cavan.[2] In 1561 it was suggested that he be created Earl of Brenny and Baron of Cavan, or Earl O'Reilly. Maolmordha refused all these offers and continued to oppose the English until his death in 1565. His death is recorded in the *Annals of Loch Cé:*

O'Raghallaigh [i.e. Maolmordha son of John] son of Cathal, the best man that ever came of his own sept, and than whom there seldom came of the race of Gaidhel Glas a better person, according to the information and knowledge of all regarding him [i.e. a man to whom God granted all the virtues at first], viz. the palm of eloquence, the palm of knowledge and learning, the palm of sense and and counsel, the palm of bounty and prowess [and it would not be wonderful that luck should attend the man of these virtues; and for these reasons he was elected chief king over the Ui Raighilligh]—was put to death while detained in captivity by the Foreigners.

The State Papers record that "Old O'Reilly died the last day of August at Ardbracaan County Meath."

In 1553 Sir Thomas Cusack, Lord Chancellor of Ireland, writing to the Duke of Northumberland relative to "The present state of Ireland" gave the following description of Breifne: "Next to the Annalie [the present county of Longford] is a large country well inhabited, called the Brenny wherein O'Rail is chief captain, who has seven sons. He may make 400 horsemen of the same name, and 1000 kerne, and 200 gallowglass. The country is divided between them, which joineth to the English Pale and upon a country called Plounkett's country, betwixt which countries there hath been divers murders, stealths, and robberies by night and day, committed."

In 1562 shortly after the accession of Elizabeth the Earl of Sussex, Lord Deputy, put forward "some reforms necessary to reduce the wild Irish to some certain kind of obedience." This was his ingenious idea:

It will be convenient to alter their states from Irish election to English succession—the election to the captainship of the country is the cause why Irishmen do keep large numbers of idle men of war, that thereby they might be the stronger, hoping by their strength to be the liker to be elected upon a vacation. These men of war, being brought up and fed with idleness cannot be restrained in time of peace from stealing and a number of other enormities. The taking away of this election and granting of estates to the heir male, will give occasion to

the captain to forsee that no man in his rule shall keep such
force as he shall be able to disturb his son in his succession,
and to others not to have the will to keep idle men of war for
that purpose, when hope of election shall be taken from
them.

In pursuance of this policy, immediately after Aodh
Connallach's election to the chieftaincy he and his
brother Edmund of Kilnacrott were forced to sign a most
humiliating agreement at Loch Sheelin. Aodh is referred
to in the Fiants of Elizabeth as Hugh Reoghe O'Reyly of
Loch Voney.

Some of the more oppressive clauses of the agreement are set out herewith:

They promise to prosecute their brothers, Cahir, Owen, and
John O'Reigly, now the Queen's rebels and to punish them
with fire and sword.

Whatever the Lords Commissioners appointed by the
Lord Deputy shall adjudicate respecting spoils between the
English parts and the inhabitants of the Brenny, O'Reigly will
perform and observe.

He shall likewise perform whatever shall be decreed by
the Deputy's commissioners between the inhabitants of the
country of Annaly and those of the country of the Brenny,
with references to injuries, both present and past.

Whereas the Lord Deputy took possession of the castle of
Tullyvyn lately in the occupation of Owen O'Reiglye and has
now committed it to Edmund O'Reiglye for the Queen's use,
O'Reiglye will take care that the same Edmund shall not har-
bour the said Owen or any other rebel, or their goods, in the
same castle or elsewhere. He shall maintain the same Edmund
in possession of the castle.

O'Reily promises to dwell on the borders of this country
and the English parts, at the pleasure of the Lord Deputy during the war and rebellion of his brothers and Shane O'Neill,
in order that the English parts may be secured by his protection against the said rebels.''

In accordance with a further clause in the agreement, "John O'Reigly, son to old O'Reilly, was delivered to the Lord Deputy as a pledge for the performance of these and all other articles, and now remaineth prisoner in the castle of Dublin."[3]

Aodh Conallach (Hugh of Tir Conaill) so called because he had been fostered with his mother's people the O'Donnells, was one of the most outstanding characters in the history of Breifne. He was a man, in many ways, larger than life: he was a great builder of castles, he built the castles of Ballinacargy or Carrick, and Belturbet (Bel Tarbet). He was married three times and had eleven sons, four of whom were legitimate.[4] His first wife was Jennet, daughter of the Betagh of Moynalty in the barony of Kells, County Meath. By her he had three sons, Seaan, Philip, and Eoghan. He married, secondly, Mary, the daughter of Sir Thomas Nugent of Carlanstown, near Finea in the county of Westmeath, who was the second son of the Baron of Delvin. They had one son, Maolmordha. His third wife was Isabella of the great family of Barnewell of Trimlestown County Meath.

Aodh's second wife, Mary was the cause of yet another of those disastrous fires which afflicted Cavan town. The incident is recorded in the *Annals of the Four Masters* under the year 1576:

The great monastery of Cavan and Cavan itself, from the great castle downwards to the river was burned by the daughter of Tomas, son of the Baron, through jealousy. There was not so much destroyed in any town among the Irish as has been in that town.[5]

According to the *Annals of Breifne* "she [Mary] set fire to a house in the town against which she had a spite, and for that reason the town was burnt on the 7th of May."

The government was now pressing forward with plans for the bringing of Breifne completely under the English law and in May 1579 the Treasurer, Sir Edward Fyton reported to Walsingham, "O'Reilly's country is to be shired, where never writ was current and almost sacrilege for any Governor to look in."[6]

It would seem that Hugh Conallach had adhered meticulously to his agreement of 1566, because in 1575 the Deputy, Sidney, reported to the Privy Council that "O'Reilly was the justest Irishman and his country the best ruled."[7] Sidney however, was doubtful about the continuance of this state of affairs and in April 1576 he reported, "O'Reilly is bed-rid; at his death there will be great trouble."[8]

A fortnight after Fyton's report Hugh, with his brothers Philip and Edmund appeared before Lord Justice Drury at the house of Sir Lucas Dillon near Kells: "They came unlooked for," says Drury, "to present unto me a submission and supplication, in behalf as well of himself as of his whole country—wherein when I found such humility and continuance of the fealty which he hath of long time professed, and in his own person performed, together with his conformity appearing therein at this time (which by report he hath been moved to before, and refused) to have his people not only framed to English manners, but also his country made shire ground and subject to law under Her Majesty's writ, weighing also his gravity in years, and good discretion in government, I thought it good to honour him with the title of knighthood, which he so humbly and thankfully received, as he vowed himself to continue and increase by all means he could, his duty and obedience unto Her Majesty."[9]

It is obvious that Hugh Conallach had now sold himself completely to the English—and he had his reward; Sir Edward Waterhouse reports to Walsingham on June 17th 1579: "The Brenny and Annally shired.

O'Reilly knighted and to be made a Baron."[10]

Father Paul Welsh in his article "Irish Chiefs and Leaders"[11] said, "In the course of the long struggle between the Tudor Governors of Ireland and the Anglo-Irish nobility of the country nothing is more remarkable than the readiness with which the leading members of the aristocracy were willing, whenever the occasion suited, to make their humble submission of life and estate, and in so doing, to disregard the interests of their neighbours and of their class as a whole, e.g. the O'Neils, O'Donnells, Maguires, MacMahons, O'Reillys, and O'Rourkes." Here we have a prime example. In fairness, however, it must be said that Hugh Connallach made some effort to protect the Religious Houses of Breifne. In 1570 when the question arose of confiscating Trinity Priory he negotiated an agreement with Elizabeth whereby he was granted the abbey with all its possessions for the term of 21 years at the rent of 55 shillings and eight pence Irish money. In the same year he obtained, on the same terms, the abbey of Drumlane at the rent of £8 . 14 . 8, but by an inquisition taken in 1584, Sir Hugh was found to be eleven and a half years in arrears.[12]

Hugh Conallach's object in negotiating these leases was to preserve these institutions until such time as a more tolerant atittude to religion prevailed; the same tactics had been tried by others at this time. As soon as he realised that there was no hope of such an outcome he stopped payment.

Sir Hugh Conallach died in 1583 and about the same time his wife Isabella Barnewell passed away. They were buried in the Monastery of Cavan. He was the last Breifne chieftain at whose funeral full Celtic honours were accorded. The Four Masters said of him: "A man who had passed his time without contests or trouble, and who had preserved Breifne from the invasions of his English and Irish enemies as long as he lived," an appreciation which seems hardly justified by events.

With almost indecent haste, following his father's death Sean Ruadh, his son by the daughter of the Beatagh, proceeded to establish his claim to the succession despite the fact that by Irish law the rightful successor was the Tanist, Edmond of Kilnacrott, brother of Aodh Conallach. Sean, finding his party too weak, repaired to Dublin to claim the support of the government where he received glowing letters from Sir Sidney Wallop and Sir Edward Waterhouse, addressed to Secretary Walsingham.

The terms of Waterhouse's letter were:

It may please your honour, this bearer John O'Reilly, fearing that his uncle and competitor in the Captaincy of the Brenny should prevail against him in England by his agents there, hath besought leave of the State here to repair to Her Majesty's presence to show his right as the eldest son of his name, legitimately born and the eldest son of the last O'Reilly, ... I do justly and truly commend him for this, not only above any O'Reilly but above all the Irish in Ireland. He has been a builder, a planter, and a sower of the earth, and, having a great part of the country has notwithstanding, kept his people from disorder.[13]

The letter from Sir Sidney Wallop was couched in the same glowing terms. Sean now crossed over to London where he was favourably received, and in June 1583, Queen Elizabeth wrote to the Lords Justices:

Her favour to the bearer Sir John O'Reilly whom she has knighted. Warrant for the succession of the country of O'Reilly according to the instructions in the Council's letters. Bill of the descent, kindred, and alliances of John O'Reilly, son of Sir Hugh O'Reilly deceased, with aids offered to him to maintain his rights against Edmond.[14]

The *Annals of Loch Cé* have the following entry under 1584: "John son of Aodh Conallach was made The O'Reilly by the Foreigners, in presence of the sons of Maolmordha O'Reilly who were senior to him; and the sons of Maolmordha destroyed the whole country through that."

Sir John O'Reilly was now an avowed supporter of the English and the Lord Deputy had got a firm grip on Breifne, and in 1584 East Breifne was converted into the county of Cavan, and West Breifne into the county of Leitrim; the latter was left in the province of Connacht but Cavan was transferred to Ulster. At the same time, in order to make the control of the country easier it was divided up into baronies with designations based on the old clan names, and the head of each barony was given a measure of autonomy independently of The O'Reilly in return for the surrender and re-grant of his estates.

The principal baronies were:

1. *Loughtee* (lucht tighe), the largest and richest, was the domain of the chief O'Reilly and contained the principal seats of Tullymongain and Loch Uachtair castles. It was occasionally known as Iochtar Tire (the lower part). As the centre of East Breifne, Cavan town and Tullymongain castle were the goal of English raids and police expeditions. The castle was occupied by Sir Hugh O'Reilly, perhaps until his death in 1583. It is likely that it was still held by Sir John O'Reilly, but the troubles of the latter end of the sixteenth century, the fortification of Cavan Abbey by an English garrison (though expelled in 1598), and the construction of another castle in the town by Walter Brady close to the abbey, all apparently, combined to cause Tullymongain to fall into disrepair. The ruin however, was still standing in 1621 and was granted with 14 acres of land, first to Sir Thomas

Rotherham and then to Lady Lambert. What ultimately happened to it is not known. Its site later became the Fair Green of the town.

Walter Brady was Constable of Cavan and though sometimes under suspicion, was strongly anglophile and became the first "sovereign" of the town when it was incorporated in 1610. Brady's castle was destroyed by Philip O'Reilly in 1596 but was re-built in 1600.

2. *Clankee* (derived from Clann-an-Caoch) was grouped round the castle of Mullagh near the Meath border. The castle is said to have been built by the sons of Glasney O'Reilly in 1485. The O'Reilly Pedigree assigns it to Conor Mor, grandson of Giolla Íosa Ruadh. Sir Hugh O'Reilly wrote from there in 1580 and it formed part of the lands escheated by the rebellion and death of Philip O'Reilly in 1598. No trace of it now remains.

3. *Clonmahon* (or Clonkeyle) was based on the castle of Crover situated on Loch Sheelin.

4. *Castlerahan,* grouped round the castle of Kilnacrott, owned by Edmond, brother of Hugh Conallach.

5. *Tullygarvey.* The only pre-Plantation castles in this barony were those of Tullyvin and Bellanacargy. The latter commanded an important ford over the River Annalee. The O'Reilly Pedigree says it was constructed by Sir Hugh Conallach, and prior to 1584 it was held by Philip O'Reilly. Some time before 1600 it became an English garrison point with a constable and six wardens. The garrison was discharged in 1610 and it was granted with a large estate to Mulmorey Oge Mc Mulmorey Mc Shane O'Reilly. He was the son of Maolmordha Alainn, "The Queen's O'Reilly." Some years later two baronies, Tullyhaw and Tullyhunco were taken out of Leitrim and incorporated in Cavan.

Two other castles are mentioned in the article from which these details are taken.[15] The castle of Lissanover was originally owned by the Magaurans but passed, about 1600 to Hugh Mc Cahir O'Reilly; at the plantation it was granted with 300 acres to Bryan Mc Shane O'Reilly. Rathdrum castle lay on a small island off a promontory of Loch Ramor. It was held by Shane Mc Hugh Mc James O'Reilly; at the plantation he was moved up country and the castle was then made the centre of the manor of Loch Ramor. It is said to have been built in the fifthteenth century by Conor Oge (of Beal-atha-an-fheada), son of Conor Mor of Mullagh.[16]

In November 1584 an indenture was completed whereby "Sir John O'Reilly is to surrender O'Reilly's and receive by grant from Her Majesty the Towghe [i.e. *tuath* or district] of the Loughtye called the barony of Cavan, and the towghe of Tullaghe Garvey now called the barony of Tullyvin."[17] He received in addition the rents from the baronies of Tullyhaw and Tullyhunco. Following on this leases were issued to the principal native landowners under the policy of surrender and re-grant. The remaining three baronies were apportioned: To Edmond of Kilnacrott and his heirs, the barony of Castlerahan; To Philip and his heirs, the barony of Inis-keen now called Clankee; To Maelmore Mc Prior and two others, the barony of Rathenarone now called Clanmahon.[18] This Maelmore was the illegitimate son of Philip the Prior, son of Aodh Conallach; the title here is misleading, he was not an ecclesiastic.

The effect of all this was that, in the case of the chief, his loyalty to the Crown was assured, since if he renounced his allegiance his lands were forfeited to the Crown, and in the case of the clan lands the individual chiefs would wield less power; also numerous freehold-ers would be created which would bring the clans di-rectly under the control of the Crown.[19] In all this the lesser members of the clan were completely ignored, and this was later to have disastrous consequences for them.

In 1590, Sir John, with a view to securing himself in

the lordship of Breifne, and in the certainty of abolishing the Tanistic succession, made a deed of feofment entailing the seignory of Breifne on his eldest son Maolmordha Breagh, otherwise known as Maolmordha Alainn (the Comely). But before long he realised that in pursuit of the Chieftainship he had made a rod for his own back. Continually harassed by succeeding Lord Deputies, he found his position unbearable and at last in 1596 he joined Hugh O'Neill in rebellion and was slain at Cavan on June 1st of that year.

Sir John O'Reilly was married twice. His first wife was the daughter of Philip O'Reilly of Iocthair Tire. They had three sons: Maolmordha, Aodh, and Cathoir. Maolmordha married Catherine Butler daughter of Sir Walter of the Beads, and niece of Thomas Dubh the celebrated Earl of Ormond. Aodh, called Captain Hugh, served in the English Army under Elizabeth and died in 1628. He was the father of Mulmorey Mc Hugh Mc Shane, Colonel of the Irish from 1642 to 1653. By his second wife, the daughter of Fergus, son of Brian O Fergail, Sir John had two sons, Seaan the Friar, and Philip father of Shane and Mulmore.

Following the death of Sir John, Hugh O'Neill promptly nominated Philip, second brother of Sir John as "O'Reilly over all Breifne" in defiance of the Government. Unfortunately, in October of the same year, Philip was involved in a quarrel with one of the O'Neills concerning the restoration of some plunder and was "accidentally" killed. Another version has it that he was slain in revenge for injuries inflicted on Ulster by Connacht. It is tempting to speculate that this way may have reference to an incident in the time of his grandfather, Maolmordha. According to the *Genealogical History of the O'Reillys*, Shane O'Neill, the Proud, surprised Maolmordha with a large host, encamping on Mullach an Mhuine eastwards from the church of Drumlane, unnoticed by anyone in Breifne; and thereupon he sent to him demanding that he pay tribute to him or else he would spoil and burn Breifne. Maolmordha answered that no man in his position had ever paid tribute to O'Neill, and he asked a stay of one week so that he might take counsel with the nobles of his land; and he promised a hundred beeves to the camp to feed them during that time. At the end of that period he attacked O'Neill in camp, defeated his host, and pursued the victory eight miles into County Monaghan. Conor and Cathaoir, two brothers of Shane were killed in this battle.

Philip himself was involved in this incident which took place in 1581. According to another account a son of Shane, Seaan Oge, was killed and another son, Conn taken prisoner.

Philip O'Reilly lived in the castle of Bellanacargy at Ballyhaise. He was married to Rose, daughter of Cu-Connacht Maguire. He had long been an implacable enemy of the English and in 1585 he was imprisoned in Dublin Castle.[20] Despite efforts to secure his release he was still in prison in September, 1590.[21] In a petition to the Privy Council he offers good security for his release and pleads that long imprisonment has impaired his health, his goods consumed, his tenants fled, his lands wasted, and his wife and children reduced to want. In December, 1591, in another petition, he offers his son as a pledge in exchange for his release. In December, 1592 we learn that his release has been ordered, and the Lord Deputy thinks that "he is likely to prove the best or the worst subject that has left Dublin Castle these forty years." It is said that his wife, an indomitable character, travelled to London and personally petitioned Queen Elizabeth for his release. Another account states that Philip escaped from Dublin Castle at Christmas, 1591, in company with Art O'Neill and the famous Red Hugh O'Donnell.

Following his nomination to the chieftaincy the Lord

Deputy reported to the Privy Council that Philip O'Reilly, contrary to his submission and the articles of agreement signed by him, has taken upon him the name of O'Reilly since the death of his brother, who has left sons to succeed him in his lands, and writes proudly to the State that he will have the Brenny brought back to the tanist law and will allow no other.[22]

At the time of his death, Philip O'Reilly's territory was the large mountainous area of Sliabh Guaire. It comprised the greater portion of the parishes of Kildrumsheridan, Drumgoon, Drung, Larah, Knockbride and portions of Killinkere and Killann. All this area became forfeit to the Crown.[23]

Following the death of Philip, Maolmordha secured the chieftaincy with the aid of the Government but his reign was a short one. He was killed at the battle of the Yellow Ford, fighting on the side of the English. One writer referred to him as a brave but degenerate member of the clan who was the first to earn the dubious title of "The Queen's O'Reilly."

"After the fall of Marshal Bagenal at this battle, on August 15th 1598, the rest of the army which he had commanded became so dispirited as to be unable to render assistance to the others. However, Maelmorus O'Reilly, surnamed 'the Comely,' ordered the vacillating to be of firm courage, and with him, to resist the enemy; that it was better to be slain fighting and avenged than to fall and be killed with impunity. Some, being animated by this exhortation of Maelmorus, particularly some of the Irish youths, his kinsmen, renew the battle, with whom as they fought, he turned him in every direction that he might aid them in their danger and distress. But the few who remained with him, being deserted by the Queen's party and surrounded by the Irish Catholics, fall covered with wounds and the comely Maelmorus, being left alone, fell fighting most valiantly."[24]

Following the death of Maolmordha Breagh, Edmund of Kilnacrott, now a very old man, was elected by the Irish as the O'Reilly but his sway only lasted for a short and stormy period. The Earl of Essex arrived in Ireland in 1599 and in a report submitted to the Privy Council at that time, stated:

In the Breany the castle of Ballindarogge, late Philip O'Reilly's . . . all the rest is rebellion. Edmond O'Reilly usurpeth the Breany, called the county of Cavan.[25]

Essex was speedily replaced by one of the most hated Englishmen who ever entered Ireland: the notorious Lord Mountjoy, whose avowed intention was to starve the whole country into submission. He later recalled that in Tyrone alone he saw 3000 bodies dead of famine. He proceeded to wage all-out war against Breifne and in 1600 he reported to Sir George Carew: "We have ransacked the Breany and left there Sir Oliver Lambert planting of a garrison, which I make no doubt but he will dispatch within a few days."[26]

This Lambert, a greedy unprincipled land grabber, was the nephew of Sir Henry Wallop, the Vice-Treasurer of Elizabeth's reign. Elizabeth had already granted Lambert extensive lands in Cavan and in 1611 James I granted him large tracts of land in Castlerahan and Clanmahon. In 1617 he was raised to the peerage and created Lord Lambert Baron of Cavan. Following his death in 1618 his widow inherited his lands and received in addition "the castle in Lough Sheelin called Castlnelough, one ruinous castle on the mountain near Cavan called O'Reyles castle, (Tullymongain) and 1500 acres extra in Clonmahon barony." In 1647 his son Charles was created Earl of Cavan.

Edmund was slain in rebellion at Cavan in 1601 and was buried in Cavan Abbey. The Four Masters describe him as:

An aged grey-headed, long memoried man, and had been quick and vivacious in his mind and intellect in his youth. He was the last chieftain of the great O'Reilly clan who maintained the Brehon system in Breifne, and the history of Breifne contains no nobler character than that of Edmund of Kilnacrott.

Edmund was married to Lady Mary Plunkett, daughter of Robert, fifth Baron of Dunsany, and by her he had three sons, Cahir, Terence, and John. He was married secondly to Lady Elizabeth Nugent, daughter of the Baron of Delvin and their sons were Charles, Myles, and Farrell. John was married to Catherine, daughter of Sir James Butler, and their son Brian, who married Mary, daughter of the Baron Dunsany and who died in 1631 was the father of the reputed Myles the Slasher. However, as will be seen later, there is considerable doubt as to the identity of this person.

Edmund's residence, the castle of Kilnacrott, was situated in the barony of Castlerahan, part of the extensive district of Cairbre Gabhra which stretched south and east of Loch Sheelin; the castle was erected in the early part of the fifteenth century on the banks of the upper Inny, the river described as the Ethne in early Irish records.

After the death of Edmund his sons remained in possession until 1609 when James I granted it to the Baroness of Delvin and her son Sir Richard Nugent together with about sixty acres of land. The Nugents held possession of the castle until the confiscations under Cromwell, when they in turn were dispossessed.

In 1661 under the terms of the Act of Settlement the castle and its lands were granted to one Abraham Clements, a soldier in the Commonwealth army.

During the second half of the eighteenth century the estate came into the possession of the Morton family where it remained until about 1840. At that time the owner was a Pierce Morton who planned considerable alterations and extensions to the castle but unfortunately, after the work had got under way he found himself unable to meet the cost and in 1850 was forced to sell the property. A few years later it was acquired by the builder who had started the alterations, and he, in order to recoup his losses, dismantled the building. No trace of the castle now remains but the site is said to be near the present Kilnacrott House occupied by the Pre-Monastratensian Canons.

Notes

1. *A History of Ireland*. Curtis.
2. C.S.P.I. (1509-1573). p 60 of 1541.
3. C.S.P.I. Carew Mss. 1566. 28 Nov.9. Eliz.
4. Gen. Hist. p 79 (5).
5. *Annals of the Four Masters*
6. C.S.P.I. 1579. p 109.
7. C.S.P.I. 1576. p 85.
8. C.S.P.I. 1576. p 92.
9. C.S.P.I. 1579. pp IV & 171.
10. Ibid. p 170.
11. Edited by Colm O' Lochlann, 1960.
12. *Monasticon Hibernicum.*1st edition (1786) p 42.
13. C.S.P.I. 1583.
14. Ibid., p 454.
15. *Castles of Cavan*. Davies.
16. B.A.S.Jn. Vol. I. 1920. p 16.
17. C.S.P.I. 1584. p 539.
18. Carew Collection, Lambeth. No. 365. Folio 19.
19. B.A.S.Jn. Vol. III. No.1. 1927. O'Connell.
20. C.S.P.I. 1586-88. p 40.
21. Poems on the O'Reillys, (Notes to). Carney.
22. C.S.P.I. 1596-7. p 35.
23. B.A.S.Jn. Vol. III.No.1. 1927. O'Connell.
24. Duffy. Jan. 1861. *The O'Reillys at Home & Abroad.*
25. John O'Donovan. L.L.D.; M.R.I.A.; quoting Philip O'Sullivan who claimed to have received the statement from 18 witnesses.
26. C.S.P.I. Carew Mss. 1599. p 299.
27. Ibid., 1601. p 42.

CHAPTER VI

The Plantation

> The moment the name of Ireland is mentioned
> the English seem to bid adieu to common
> feeling, common prudence, and common sense,
> and to act with the barbarity of tyrants and
> the fatuity of idiots.
>
> —Revd. Sidney Smith (1741-1845)

With the accession of James I to the English throne Ireland had great hopes of renewed peace and religious tolerance. But the discovery of the Gunpowder Plot resulted in severe penal laws being enacted against Roman Catholics. The leaders of the Gaelic aristocracy, O'Neill, Earl of Tyrone, and O'Donnell found themselves increasingly harassed, and eventually decided to leave Ireland; and on September 14th 1607, Tyrone, Tyrconnell, and his brother; Maguire and others; ninty-nine in all of the leading men of the north, sailed from Lough Swilly and sought refuge in Spain. With their departure we may truly say there came to an end that Milesian aristocracy which had lorded over Ireland from the dawn of history.[1]

One factor concerned in precipitating this "Flight of the Earls" was the rebellious intrigue between Richard, Nugent, 10th Baron Delvin, and Lord Howth, his kinsman. At this time Loch Uachtair castle was owned by Nugent. Having been imprisoned in Dublin Castle he escaped and fled to Cloch Uachtair. After taking to the mountains and living rough for three months, he surrendered, was taken to England and eventually pardoned.

Following the flight of O'Neill and O'Donnell plans were formulated for the plantation of Ulster, including the County of Cavan. The chief architect of the plan was Sir John Davies. He appeared in Ireland in 1603 as Solicitor General and at once set about making a detailed investigation into the custom and legality of land holding in Ireland with a view to getting possession of it in the name of the Crown. The flight of the Earls left the way open for this; indeed Davies is on record as having said "Saint Patrick banished the worms out of Ireland; it was left for King James to bring about the departure of the men full of poison as well."

Davies' first visit to Cavan was in 1606, when he was accompanied by three others of the same kidney—the Lord Deputy Chichester, Sir Oliver Lambert, and Sir Garret Moore. They spent a week in what Chichester described as "the poor towne bearing the name of Cavan, seated betwixt many small hills."[2] "The Brenie, Breny Oreylye, or O'Reilly's county of Cavan had up to this time been little better than a den of thieves, infesting the two counties of East and West Meath with continued spoils and robberies."[3]

On their return to Dublin Davies wrote to Lord Salisbury: "His Lordship [Chichester] in this journey hath cut off the three heads of that hydra of the north, namely, McMahon, Maguire, and O'Reilly; for these three names of chiefry with their Irish duties and exactions shall be utterly abolished: the customs of tanistry and gavilkind shall be clearly extinguished, all the possessions shall descend and be conveyed according to the course of the common law."[4]

In 1606 a commission was directed to Sir Garret Moore and others to ascertain what lands were to come to the Crown in the County of Cavan, in pursuance whereof, an inquisition found that Philip O'Reilly (the rebel of 1596) was seized in the 38th year of Elizabeth, of the entire region or territory of Breifne O'Reilly, containing seven entire baronies, into which, on the day that Philip died, Edmond O'Reilly entered, and levying open war on the Queen, was also slain; that the said Sir John O'Reilly had claimed the said county by tanistry and was for a time received into the Queen's favour, but that he adhered to Tyrone and died a rebel.

Such a verdict was a foregone conclusion since it was brought in by a packed jury containing only three Irishmen, but having several English servitors (who later received estates), and Fleming, Tyrell, and Nugent, who had already obtained a foothold in the county. They added that no other natives had freehold rights, so they could be dispossessed at will.[5]

In 1609 the complete plan was issued. In the whole of Ulster some 500,000 acres of "profitable land" were thrown open to settlers; English and Scottish undertakers were invited to take estates of 1,000, 1,500, or 2,000 acres, to hold of the Crown in socage. They were to be English, or inland (i.e. lowland) Scots and civil men well affected in religion. A second rank of grantees were called "servitors" on less favourable terms, who were generally Scots. All were compelled to take the Oath of Supremacy admitting the king to be the Head of the Church. A third rank consisted of "Natives" who received grants from the Crown but were not required to take the oath. Undertakers and servitors were, after a period, to pay a head rent to the Crown of £5. 6. 8. for every 1000 acres. Neither of them might alienate the fee to the Irish, but the servitors might take Irish tenants at £8 for every 1000 acres, i.e. they must pay a heavier rent if they took Irish tenants. The natives were to pay a heavier head rent, viz, £10. 13. 4. for every 1000 acres, or in proportion, and might take tenants.[6]

However, the descendants of Sir John O'Reilly and of his brothers were restored to considerable tracts of land. The following are mentioned in Pynnar's Survey:

1. Shane Mc Philip O'Reilly who got 900 acres in the precinct of Castlerahan.

2. Mulmore Mc Philip O'Reilly, 1000 acres called Ittery Outra in the precinct of Tullygarvey.

3. Captain Hugh O'Reilly, 1000 acres called Liscannor in the precinct of Tullygarvey.

4. Mulmore Oge O'Reilly, 3000 acres in the same.

5. Mulmorey Mc Hugh O'Reilly, 2000 acres called Commet in the precinct of Clanmahon

6. Philip Mac Tirlagh, 300 acres called Wateragh in the same.

It will be remembered that Shane and Mulmore Mc Philip were the sons of Philip, son of Sir John O'Reilly by his second wife, the daughter of Fergus, son O Fergail.

On the occasion of this commission no less than fifty-two persons of the family of O'Reilly who were proprietors of considerable tracts of land were attainted. The persons named above were alone deemed worthy of being restored to portions of their ancient estates.

The ordinary natives were naturally alarmed at the implications of the addendum to the commisioners' verdict and at a meeting in the public sessions house in Cavan town they put it to Davies that the freeholders of Cavan had estates of inheritance which had not been forfeited. Davies replied in a long speech which for sheer hypocrisy is unsurpassed in the long history of double dealing which characterised the English Crown's relations with the native Irish.

Davies said that he was glad of an opportunity to make things clear: "The King," he said, "being the most just prince living, would not dispossess any of his subjects wrongfully; but this was not wrongful dispossession. The King, in law, in conscience, and in honour, had the right to dispose of the escheated counties as he saw fit. He had the right in law because he was the lord paramount and so might dispose of the estates of tenants which 'doth fail and determine.'

"In particular he was the lord paramount of Cavan because the chieftainship of the O'Reillys had been abolished and because the two principal O'Reillys had been killed in rebellion and their lands had been attainted to the Crown. The claimants had no estates of inheritance because 'neither their chiefries nor their tenancies did ever descend to a certain heir.' The estates of Chieftains and tanists had been adjudged no estates in law, but only a transitory and scrambling possession. Therefore the claimants could show no common law title to their estates. Moreover, even by Brehon law the King, having the supreme chiefry, could dispose of the land as he wished. Therefore, he continued, as well by Irish custom as by English law the King might at his pleasure seize these lands and dispose thereof. How far however, in conscience and honour, might he remove the ancient tenants and bring in strangers among them? Why, as far as conscience and honour were concerned the King was bound to take the course proposed. He was bound to use all lawful and just courses to reduce the people from barbarism to civility. Ulster could be civilized only by plantation, for if the people were allowed to remain in possession of their land, as they possessed it from time immemorial, they would never, to the end of the world, build houses, make townships or villages, or manure or improve the land as it ought to be. It would be altogether wrong to suffer so good and fruitful a country to lie waste like a wilderness."[7]

As a result of the Plantation Ulster finally became a province almost entirely Protestant as regards the landowners and mainly so as regards the population, and it is reckoned that by 1641, of the 3,500,000 acres in the six counties, the Protestants owned 3,000,000 acres and the Catholics the rest. But even this proportion was to be reduced after 1660, and after 1690, scarcely anything of the Gaelic and Catholic aristocracy remained.[8]

After The Plantation

With the advent of Charles I all Ireland hoped for better things. He had a Catholic wife and was believed to be sympathic to the Old Religion; but the start of his reign was ominous. He promised certain "Graces" in return for a payment of £20,000. The money was paid but the promises were never kept. Worse still he virtually handed over control of the country to two bigoted puritanical individuals, the lords justices Borlase and Parsons. Their avowed object was to drive the Irish into rebellion and seize their lands for the Crown.

The plan succeeded only too well and a full scale rising took place in 1641. In Cavan the two leaders of the Confederate Catholics were Colonel Philip O'Reilly, son of Captain Hugh, the younger son of Sir John O'Reilly, and his kinsman Maelmore O'Reilly, the son of Emonn, son of Lucas, son of Maelmore, son of Hugh Conallach; the latter lived in Lismore Castle at Crossdoney.[9] Colonel Philip was living at Ballynacargy Castle in 1653; as a young man he served for some time in the Spanish army, but returned to Ireland at some date prior to 1641. He raised a brigade of 1200 men composed chiefly of his name and family, and served with distinction as Lieutenant General in the Confederacy. He married Rose, sister of Owen Roe O'Neill, and co-operated throughout the war with that great leader. He was attainted in 1642 and again, in 1652 was further denounced under Cromwell's Act. Being obliged to expatriate himself he retired with his brigade to the Netherlands where he served in the Spanish army for about three years. He died in 1655 and was buried in the Monastery of Louvain. He had a son, Hugh Roe who was slain by the Parliamentary forces in Cavan in 1651, leaving by his wife Margaret, daughter of Conor O'Brien Lord Viscount Clare, an only son, Hugh Oge, who was drowned on passage from Spain. In him the race of Colonel Philip became extinct. According to O'Connell[10] Colonel Philip also had a daughter Eibhlin who was the mother of Primate Hugh MacMahon.

The Problem of Myles the Slasher

Myles was the great hero figure of the 1641 war but considerable doubt exists as to who he really was. O'Donovan[11] gives an account of his last great stand at the bridge of Finea in the summer of 1644, when confronting the Scots under General Munroe. According to this, Myles was encamped at Granard with Lord Castlehaven, leader of the Confederate forces. The latter ordered him to proceed, with a chosen detachment of horse, to defend the bridge of Finea against the Scots, then bearing down on the main army with a very superior force. Myles was slain at the head of his troops, fighting bravely on the middle of the bridge; a popular ballad[12] thus describes the scene:

> . . . He fought till the dead and the dying
> Heaped high on the battlements lay.
> He fell, but the foot of the foreman
> Passed not o'er the Bridge of Finea.

Tradition has it that during the action Myles encountered a colonel of the Scots in single combat who laid open his cheek with a blow of his sword, but Myles, whose jaws were stronger than a smith's vise, held fast the Scotsman's sword between his teeth till he cut him down, but the main body of the Scots pressing on them, Myles was left dead on the field. His body was discovered the following day and conveyed to the Monastery of Cavan where he was interred in the tomb of his ancestors.

A tradition locally remembered at Crosserlough says that when Myles was killed his head was cut off and brought to Cavan where it was impaled on the railings of Cavan church. Tradition further states that a man named Flynn from Denn parish took the head from Cavan and brought it to Crosserlough where it was kept for years in a niche in the outer wall of the ruined church.

According to O'Donovan Myles married Catherine, daughter of Charles O'Reilly of Leitrim. Their three sons, John, Edmond, and Philip are mentioned in the O'Reilly Pedigree.[13] The same source states that Myles was the son of Brian, son of John, son of Edmond of Kilnacrott. It also appears from a document dated 1716 that Myles had two daughters, Honora, and Rose. Their three sons and two daughters were said to be still living 73 years after the battle of Finea. There is another tradition which states that after the 1641 rebellion, which Myles survived, he lived for some time on the island of Clough-inis-Tork in Lough Finvoy, County Leitrim where the people retained a vivid recollection of him.

All of this emphasizes the doubt which existed as to who Myles really was. The late Fr. Paul Walsh made an exhaustive enquiry into the identity of "The Slasher."[14] He admits that there is mention of a colonel in charge of the defence of the bridge of Finea but for his name we have to go to the *Aphorismical Discovery*, Part 1, p. 83:[15] "Our Council general undervaluing all difficulty, commanded Colonel John Butler, Mountgarrett's brother, now General of the Horse in Leinster, to march in all haste to FYNEA and make good that passage."

Lord Castlehaven himself has left a detailed account of the circumstances surrounding the battle of Finea:

"the first rendezvous I made in order to this field was about Midsummer 1644 at Granard in the County of Longford where I had appointed about 3,000 Horse and Foot with two or three field pieces to meet me, intending there to have expected the coming up of the whole army; which might be in four or five days time; for O'Neill was encamped at Portlester, and the rest marching as ordered. My spyes that met me at the rendezvous and came in last, all agreed they had left the enemy near a certain mountain three miles off; that they were 17,000 strong with one and twenty days provisions, no cannon or other baggage, and were ready to march.

"I thought myself pretty secure for that night but before one day, one from Cavan [which was about 12 miles distant] assured me that he had left the whole army of the enemy there, and that their Horse and Dragoons would be with me in the morning. On this advice I packed off as fast as I could and gained Portlester, having ordered the rest of the army to come thither; and at the instant commanded a colonel with 5 or 600 of Foot and 100 Horse to defend the bridge of Fineagh, that I might not be pursued. It was of stone, and a castle at our end. I sent with him shovels, picks, and axes, and spades, with plenty of ammunition. The enemy, according to my information, came at sun rising into the camp I had left and showed themselves next day, before that bridge; but my unfortunate colonel sent over his horse to skirmish, and when they were far enough out, on a sudden the enemy mingled with them, which was the cause our Foot could do nothing, but through fear to kill their own, left bridge, castle and all free for the enemy."[16] No mention of an O'Reilly here; and indeed, far from "the foot of a foeman passed not o'er the bridge of Finea" the defenders ran away from the place, and the enemy poured over into County Westmeath and destroyed all Finea as well as Carolstown in the immediate neighbourhood.

Belling's *History* is in agreement with both these accounts: ". . .Advertisement coming to him [Castlehaven] from a colonel of the enemy who wished well to the king, Castlehaven immediately retreats to Portlester . . . and immediately sent Colonel John Butler with four or five hundred Horse and Foot to defend the bridge of Finea."[17]

There is also a contemporary account of the battle in the Irish Journal of Friar O'Mellan which gives a list of the Confederation officers killed at the battle. In none of these accounts does the name of Myles O'Reilly appear.

Professor Carney states[18] that the first to use the term "Slasher" was the Chevalier O'Gorman in his work on the O'Reilly family[19] where he identifies him with Maolmordha, son of Seaan, head of the Kilnacrott branch of the family; Professor Carney goes on to say; I have read all the unpublished Gaelic material on the O'Reilly mentioned in this work, a great deal of it is 17th century work; none of these sources mentioned a Maolmordha (Myles) with a Gaelic epithet corresponding with "Slasher." Myles is popularly supposed to have been slain at Finea but the only O'Reilly which these sources mention as slain there is one Aodh Ruadh.

I think there is little doubt that Professor Carney has provided the solution to the problem of who, if indeed he really existed, was the famous O'Reilly commonly known as "Myles the Slasher." He quotes an anecdote by Dr Fitzimons, the original author of the *Genealogical History of the O'Reillys*. This author related the sword incident as concerning Maolmordha, son of Emonn, son of Maolmordha, son of Aodh Conallach, known as "The Renowned Colonel" of the Cromwellian Wars; at Cros Ribach, leading a cavalry troop of ten, he seized, slew, or put to flight, 150 of the English cavalry. He was at the engagements at Benburb, Lios na Sraon, and Sliabh Roisil, at which latter encounter, the incident of the sword took place. He later went to Spain, where he was honoured by the King and by his son, and later, by the King of France. Finally he went to Flanders, became ill there and died in the monastery of the Irish Capuchins in Charleville, in 1670.

Professor Carney points out[20] that Dr Fitzimons is here giving information about a man who was a contemporary and whom he doubtless knew personally: "It is easy to see a possible origin of the term 'Slasher'. From the incident with the Scots colonel [actually a Captain Calbret], Maolmordha could be referred to as Maolmordha an Chloidhimh, i.e. Maolmordha of [the incident] of the Sword." Such a reference could have suggested the English Myles the Slasher, despite the fact that reference to the context would rather suggest "Myles the Slashed."

Fr. Paul Walsh suggests that although the Chevalier O'Gorman derived the story of the Slasher from Dr. Fitzimon's manuscript he deliberately ascribed the incident to the ancestor of the O'Reilly for whom he was compiling the Pedigree.

The Renowned Colonel was Sheriff of Cavan in 1641 but on the outbreak of war he and his father threw off their allegiance to the English and the Colonel fought throughout the war from 1642 to 1653. His father appears to have ceased to take an active part after 1642; he died in 1647. The Colonel was married to a sister of Owen Roe O'Neill. He had a son, Maolmordha Oge, about whom nothing further is known.

In the *Book of Surveys*, Colonel Myles is referred to as Miles Riley, Irish Papist, and recorded as having possessed, in 1641, the following properties; in the parishes of Denn and Kilmore, in the barony of Clanmahon; Kilmannan, Drumcoe, Covett (Kevitt), Shannow, and Rabrachan.

Notwithstanding the conclusive evidence against the presence of "The Slasher" at Finea a handsome monument to his memory has been erected in the main street of that village.

The war of 1641-53 had a disastrous effect on the

Front and back views of the Slasher Memorial at Finea village, in honor of the controversial Myles O'Reilly, "the Slasher."

KE,S
CLARKE'S
SPECIAL
NUGGET
PLUG
HAND
CUT
TOP ACC

population of the country. It was followed by confiscations, pestilence, and famine; large numbers of the defeated forces went abroad and entered the armies of France and Spain, but in addition, large numbers were sold into slavery and shipped abroad. The government entered into a contract with the merchants of Bristol, and men, women, and young girls were forcibly seized and sold as slaves. Petty gives the number thus sold as 8,000 but double that number would be nearer the truth. He calculated that 616,000 people had perished as a result of the wars.[21] Needless to say Breifne was one of the places most seriously affected by this holocaust.

Before the war ended the great leader, Owen Roe was stricken by a lingering illness. He retired to Loch Uachtair Castle where he died on November 6th 1649; some say his end was hastened by poison administered by government agents. He was buried in the Franciscan Monastery of Cavan.

Cromwell's last act of villany in Breifne was the destruction of Loch Uachtair Castle, in 1653. O'Donovan records that in his time "there was a small old road leading to the castle through the townlands of Corracanwy and Inishgonnell, still called 'Cromwell's Road'; it was said to have been made by him for the purpose of drawing his cannon to destroy it."[22]

Notes

1. *A History of Ireland*. Curtis.
2. C.S.P.I. 1603-6. p 565.
3. Ibid., p 561.
4. Ibid., p 537.
5. *A History of Ireland*. Curtis.
6. "Sir John Davies in Cavan." *Breifne*. 1960. G.A. Hayes Mc Coy. M.A.; Ph.D.; D. Litt.; M.R.I.A.
7. *A History of Ireland*. Curtis.
8. *Irish Book Lover*. Vol 22. 1934.
9. Ibid.

10. Duffy. Feb. 1861.
11. "The Bridge of Fynea. William Collins. New York. 1876.
12. Gen. Hist. p 84. (11),3.
13. I.E.R. Vol. XV. 1935.
14. A Contemporary History of Affairs in Ireland from 1641–1652. Edited by Gilbert.
15. *History of the Irish Confederation and War in Ireland*. Vol. III.
16. *Gen.* Hist. Introduction.
17. *The O'Reilly Pedigree*. O'Gorman. 1786.
18. B.A.S. Jn. Vol III No. 1. 1927.

CHAPTER VII

The Descendants of Sir John O'Reilly and Edmond of Kilnacrott

Sir John O'Reilly had a younger son, Hugh Mc Shane O'Reilly otherwise known as Captain Hugh. He was a serving officer with the English army and, as recorded earlier, received a grant of 1,000 acres at the Plantation. Hugh's son, Colonel Philip who lived at Ballinacargy, we have already referred to. He had another son, Mulmorey Mc Hugh Mc Shane who played an important part at the siege of Clonmel during the 1641 war; he also distinguished himself on an occasion when he was surrounded on all sides by the English on Ballyconnell Mountain but fought his way out and continued to resist the English until he surrendered in 1653.

Mulmorey's son, Emonn (Edmund) Buidhe served as a youth in France with the King's Life Guards. He returned to Ireland in 1688 with King James II by whom he was appointed Colonel of Infantry and Lord Lieutenant of Cavan. He was involved in an encounter between the Duke of Berwick and Colonel Wolesley in which a number of people including a Captain O'Reilly were slain. He was also prominent at the battle of the Boyne, the siege of Limerick, and of Athlone. He was present at the siege of Galway and was one of the hostages for its surrender. In the articles of capitulation a special clause was inserted for the protection of his wife's mother and family, and also for the family of his brother, Lieutenant Luke O'Reilly. After the fall of Limerick Emonn, along with many others, retired to France where he died in 1693. His wife was Joan, daughter of Brian Offerall of Moate in the county of Longford. He had two sons, Owen, who served in France in Dorrington's, later, Dillon's Regiment; and Myles.

Owen married, at St. Germain, the daughter of Colonel Felix O'Reilly. He died in 1735 leaving two sons, Philip and Edmond. O'Callaghan states[1] on the authority of information given by a Mr. O'Reilly of Antillies to a Mr. de la Ponce, that Philip went to Scotland to support the cause of Prince Charles Edward Stuart, where he was captured by the enemy and burned alive. Edmond, who joined the Irish Brigade in France, was a captain in Lally's Regiment in 1757. In the following year he was created Knight of St. Louis. Later he was a captain in Dillon's Regiment and in 1773 he retired with the rank of Lieutenant Colonel. He was still living in Paris at the time of the French Revolution.

Emonn Buidhe's son, Myles, succeeded him and was called "Colonel" by courtesy. With his death the last of the possessions of the O'Reillys passed away, if we except the barren rocks at Drumheel near Ballanagh, which being worthless to anyone, were left in the possession of the Beltrasna branch of the family. The "Colonel's son, Edmond, settled on a farm in Coronary near Cloone; Brian, son of this Edmond took the townland of Illaundartry on a lease for the term of the life of George III, at the end of which time unsuccessful attempts were made to evict him. As far as is known this was the end of the line of Sir John O'Reilly."[2]

The Line of Edmund of Kilnacrott

Maolmordha the son of Brian and great grandson of Edmund of Kilnacrott had, as mentioned earlier, three sons, John, Philip, and Edmond. The most important of these was John, later known as Colonel John, who was the first to drop the O'! He was born in 1646. He owned the estates of Clonlyn and Garryroebuck in the parish of Kilbride, County Cavan, and also had a residence at Ballymacadd in County Meath. His wife was Margaret, daughter of Owen O'Reilly. In 1689 he was elected a Knight of the Shire for County Cavan in the Parliament held in Dublin in that year.

Colonel John was a staunch supporter of King James and raised a regiment of dragoons at his own expense for the war of 1690. Incidentally it may be mentioned that in King James's army, Colonel Edmond O'Reilly's regiment of infantry included thirty-three officers, and Colonel Mahon's regiment, sixteen officers named Reilly or O'Reilly. Colonel John was present at the siege of Derry and fought two engagements with Colonel Wolesley, commander of the garrison at Belturbet whom he signally defeated. The latter gentleman was also heavily defeated in a battle in Cavan town, the last affliction suffered by that unhappy place.

Colonel John also fought at the battle of the Boyne and at Aughrim. Although he was outlawed for high treason in June 1692 he was included in the articles of capitulation of Limerick whereby he retained his property and was allowed to carry arms. He had five sons and two daughters. His sons were, Conor, Myles, Brian, Owen, and Thomas. His daughters were Catherine and Mary.[3]

Colonel John died on February 17th, 1716 or 1717 according to the new style of reckoning; he was buried in the graveyard alongside the old parish church of Kildrumfertan (Cill Druim Feartain, i.e. The Church of the ridge of the graves) a few miles north west of the town of Kilnaleck. In the cemetery are two large tombs about nine feet apart. One is covered with a massive slab about 7 foot by 3 feet 6 inches on which is the following inscription:

The ruined church of Kildrumfertan near the town of Kilnaleck, Cavan, Ireland. "Cill Druim Feartain" means "Church of the ridge of graves."

HERE LIETH ENTOMBED THE
BODY OF COLONEL JOHN
REILLY WHO WAS ELECTED
KNIGHT OF THE SHIRE FOR
THE COUNTY OF CAVAN IN
THE YEAR 1689 AND DEPARTED
THIS LIFE 17 DAY OF FEBY 1716-17
AND LEFT 5 SONS AND 2 DAUGHTERS

Above this inscription is a coat of arms of the O'Reillys now somewhat difficult to decipher. There are two lions rampant, combatant supporting a dexter hand couped at the wrist. Underneath is the motto *Dum Spiro Spero;* on an upright slab at the north end of the tomb is another inscription:

THIS TOMB WAS
ERECTED BY

CONOR, MYLES
BRYAN, OWEN
AND THOMAS
REILLY, GENT
LEMEN TO COMM
EMORATE THEIR
FATHER COLONEL
JOHN REILLY
WHO DIED FEBY
THE 17TH 1716-17
AGED 70 YEARS

On the upright slab at the south end is the inscription:

SACRED TO THE MEMORY OF
THE
O'REILLYS
OF THE HOUSE OF
BALTRASNA.

The second tomb is somewhat larger, the covering slab measuring 8' by 4'. The inscription on this tomb is so much worn that it is indecipherable, but according to Dr. O'Connell in a detailed article in *Breifne* (1962), it is as follows:

Here lieth the body of Colonel
John O'Reilly who was elected Knight
of the Shier for the County of Cavan in the
year 1689. He departed this life the 17th Feb 1716
leaving 5 sons and 2 daughters.
Also the body of his eldest son Bryan O'Reilly Esq.
late of Ballinrink in this county who
died the 6th September 1749 aged 72 years
and of Margaret O'Reilly wife to the said Bryan
obit the 30th November 1755 aged 72 years
On the 4th of Feb 1775 Myles O'Reilly Esq
late of the City of Dublin eldest son of

The tombs at the old church of Kildrumfertan, each of which curiously enough claims by its inscription to be the tomb of Colonel John O'Reilly who died in either 1716 or 17.

the above Bryan Departed this life
in the 68th year of his age and on the 5th of
said month Saragh O'Reilly his wife in
the 57th year of her age. This small token
of Esteem to their memories was Erected
by John Alex O'Reilly Esq Dowell
O'Reilly and Matthew O'Reilly sons of
the above Myles O'Reilly.

On this tomb is depicted the more conventional coat of arms, crest, and motto of the family; two lions rampant, combatant supporting a sinister hand couped at the wrist. The crest is an oak tree out of a ducal coronet, a snake entwined around the trunk. The motto is *Fortudine et Prudentia.*

It is a curious thing that the name of Colonel John appears on both tombs so that it is impossible to say under which his body lies.

The seal of Colonel John is preserved in the Irish Royal Academy. All his children died without issue except Myles, Bryan, Owen and Thomas. His eldest son, known as Captain Conor, married, in 1692, Mary, daughter of Luke O'Reilly of Tonogh, near Kilnacrott. He was outlawed for high treason on June 8th 1692 and died in May 1723.

On his death the second son, Myles, succeeded to his father's estates. He was a linen merchant in Dublin and apparently, a successful businessman. He resuscitated the family estates which were in a poor financial state at his father's death. He married, in 1698, Elizabeth Barnewell, a member of a distinguished County Meath family, by whom he had four sons, John the Counsellor, Myles, Dominic, and Francis.[4] John, born in 1702, was a barrister of the Middle Temple and of some eminence as a pleader. On the death of his father in 1731 he succeeded to some of his grandfather's estates, and in the same year he was appointed by the Irish Catholics to approach the government for some amelioration of the penal code. This assignment involved him in heavy financial losses and in 1765 he sold his estates to his cousin James, son of Colonel John's youngest son, Thomas. He retired to London where he died in 1767. Myles's daughter, Mary, married Philip Tuite of Newcastle; and Margaret married Walter Dowdall of Cloune, County Meath.[5]

Colonel John's third son, Bryan, served in his father's regiment during the Jacobite wars. He was married to Margaret, daughter of Colonel Luke MacDowell of Mantua, County Roscommon.[6] They had six sons, Myles Reilly of Tullystown, Alexander, Matthew, Luke, Conor, and Edmond.

Bryan lived at Ballinrink in the parish of Killeagh, County Meath where he gave a site for the church, now in ruins. A tablet which was in the church at one time, carried the following inscription:

PRAY FOR THE SOULES
OF
BRYAN AND MARGARET REILY
LATE OF BALEIRINK
IN THIS PARISH
WHERE THEY LIVED 44 YEARS
MAN AND WIFE
BLESSED WITH EVERY CONJUGAL
HAPPINESS
AND IN THE GOOD WILL
OF THEIR NEIGHBOURS
THEY DID ALL THE GOOD THEY COULD
AND INJURED NO MAN
HE DIED THE 6TH SEPTEMBER 1749
AGED 72 YEARS
SHE DIED THE 30TH NOVEMBER 1755
AGED 72 YEARS
REQUIESCANT IN PACE.

Both were interred in the family burial ground at Kildrumfertan near Kilnaleck. All Brian's sons died without issue except Myles. He had a small estate at Tullystown County Westmeath, near the Cavan border. He was married to Sarah, daughter of William Fitzsimons of Garadice County Meath. They had three sons, John Alexander, Dowell, and Matthew. They also had a daughter, Margaret, who married the Baron de Bellegarde of Toulouse in France.[7] Myles died on February 4th, 1775 aged 68. His wife died on the following day at the age of 57.

Myles's eldest son, John Alexander, married Mary Lalor of Cranagh, County Tipperary. He joined the Spanish army in 1767 in the famous Hibernia Regiment and retired from active service in 1787; he died in England in 1801 aged 54. Dowell, the second son was married twice. His first wife, whom he married in 1775, was the daughter of John O'Connor of Dublin, but she died the same year without issue. In 1780 he married

Elizabeth, the daughter of James Knox of Moyne Abbey, County Mayo. He was the first of the family to adopt the State religion, as did his son, Myles John, for a time. In 1804 Dowell purchased the sub-lease of Heath House near Port Laoighise where he resided until his death in 1808. He left four sons the eldest of whom, Myles John, qualified as a barrister and was called to the Irish Bar though he never practised. He was married to Elizabeth Anne de la Poer Beresford of County Waterford, by whom he had three sons. The eldest, Myles George, died in 1912. Myles John himself died at Naples in 1857 aged 77.

Myles John devoted a great deal of time to the study of Irish Genealogy and particularly of the O'Reilly family. He was an intimate friend of the antiquarian John O'Donovan with whom he corresponded over a period of twenty years. His papers and correspondence are now preserved in the Royal Irish Academy. He also possessed a collection of family portraits which are now in the library of Trinity College, Dublin. Two of them are reproduced here.

A daughter of Myles John, Margaret, married William O'Reilly of Knock Abbey, County Louth. They had a son, Myles, William Patrick, who, in 1859 married Ida, the daughter of Edward Jerningham. He was educated at St. Cuthbert's Wishaw County Durham, and at London University where he gained the degree of B.A. Some time later he obtained the degree of L.L.D. at Rome. He joined the Louth Rifles Militia and later, was invited to Rome by Pope Pius IX where he entered the Papal service with the rank of Major. He defended Spoleto against the Piedmontese troops in 1860. On his return to Ireland he was elected M.P. for Longford in 1862 and was also appointed a magistrate for the counties of Louth and Dublin. He died on February 2nd, 1880 and was buried in the family burial ground at Philipstown near Knock Abbey.

Colonel John O'Reilly, the man buried in two tombs according to the tombstone inscriptions at Kildrumfertan Church.

The fourth son of Colonel John, Owen, had three sons, James, Peter, and George, but no details exist concerning them.

Thomas, the fifth and youngest son of Colonel John married, in 1691, Rose, the daughter of Luke MacDowell of Mantua. He joined his father's regiment and served in the campaigns of 1689 to 1691 and was present at the siege of Limerick. He was included in the articles of capitulation and thus secured his property. He lived at Baltrasna near Oldcastle in the County Meath where he died in 1756. He had five sons, Patrick, Philip the Friar, James, Thomas and Conor, according to the *O'Reilly Pedigree.*[8] Of these, Patrick and Conor died without issue. Strangely his most famous son, Count Alexander, does not appear in the *Pedigree,* and according to *Burke's Landed Gentry* there were two other sons, Dominick and Nicholas both of whom entered the Spanish service. His son James, born in 1718 inherited the Baltrasna estate. He married Catherine, daughter of Philip Tuite of Newcastle. He died in 1786. It appears that Thomas also had a daughter who married a Captain Adams. The latter assumed the name of O'Reilly and from them descended the O'Reillys of Belmont.

Count Alexander, the youngest son of Thomas, was born in 1722. He was seventh in descent from Edmond of Kilnacrott. He entered the Spanish service as a lieutenant in the Irish Brigade where he had such a distinguished career that he was given the title of Count. In 1757 he joined the Austrian Army where he distinguished himself against the Prussians at Hoch Kirchin. Later he returned to the Spanish service and was active in the battles of Bergen, Minden, and Corbach. On the outbreak of war between Spain and Portugal, Count Alexander served with the rank of Lieutenant General, and in 1762 defeated the Portuguese troops before Chaves.

With the declaration of peace in 1763 the Count's active military service came to an end but before that he had re-modelled the Spanish Army and introduced much needed disciplinary reforms. In 1765 he was instrumental in saving the life of Charles III during a riotous outbreak in Madrid. Following this he was pro-

Count Alexander O'Reilly as a child. He later gained his title as a result of his valiant service in the Spanish Army.

moted to the rank of Field Marshal and was sent to Havana as second in command. In June 1768 he was appointed Governor of Louisiana; later, on his return to Spain, he was made "Generalissimo of His Catholic Majesty's Forces," Govenor of Madrid, and Inspector General of Infantry.

Such a meteoric rise to fame could not but arouse

Field Marshal Count Alexander O'Reilly, who as a result of saving the Spanish King Charles III's life, moved up rapidly in the Spanish Service; at one time Governor of Madrid.

the jealousy of his military colleagues, who succeeded in having him removed from his appointments. However, he was held in high esteem by Charles III who appointed him Govenor of Cadiz and Captain General of Andalusia.

The continuing jealousy of the Spanish officers forced him to retire soon afterwards. He was a generous patron of the Irish College at Salamanca; according to the narrative of an Irish priest who met him there, his great ambition was to lead a Spanish army against England, to land in Ireland and abolish tyranny, and "the very first thing he swore to do was to burn to the ground his ancestral home, polluted by conforming kinsmen whom he swore he would put to the sword."[9]

Count Alexander was married to Donna Rosa Las Casas, by whom he had four sons, Don Conor, a lieutenant in the Regiment of Hibernia, who died in 1751; Don Dominic, Lieutenant General, who died in 1796; Peter Paul, who succeeded as Count; and Don Nicholas, Brigadier General, Governor of Mon Juich. He died in Barcelona in 1797, leaving by his wife, Anne Mary Tichbourne, a son, Don Antonio, Lieutenant Colonel who was living at La Plaza, Cadiz in 1812.

In 1786 Count Alexander commisioned Chevalier Thomas O'Gorman to compile a history of the O'Reilly family in connection with the forthcoming marriage of his son Peter Paul to the Countess Buenavista. The title of the work was *Genealogia antiquissimae O'Reilliorum Familiae*. The genealogy, in Latin, and on vellum, with an English translation, was sent to the Count by Dowell O'Reilly of Heath House. The Latin document was deposited in the Spanish Archives, and the Count retained the translation in his private library. A copy of the translation was, and presumably still is, in the Office of Arms in Dublin Castle; from it Edward O'Reilly made a transcript (with addenda), which, in 1851 was in the possession of John O'Donovan. Bryan Geraghty, who in collaboration with Philip MacDermott, published in 1845 a translation of the *Four Masters*, appears to have had a copy of the *Genealogia*.[10]

The Count died on March 23rd, 1794 at the little town of Chinchilla in the Albacete province of Central

134

Spain. He is commemorated by the Calle O'Reilly, one of the principal streets in Havana.

Oddly enough the Count is also commemorated in Lord Byron's poem, "Don Juan." In canto CXVIII the heroine, Donna Julia declares: ". . . Is it for this that General Count O'Reilly Who took Algiers declares I used him vilely?" A footnote by the editor of Byron's works points out however, that here Donna Julia made a mistake. Count O'Reilly did not take Algiers—but Algiers very nearly took him; he and his army and fleet retreated with great loss, and not much credit, from before that city, in the year 1775.

Another distinguished branch of the O'Reilly family lived at Ballinlough County Meath. They are said to be descended from Felim, grandson of Giolla Iosa Ruadh, who was treacherously captured at Trim in 1447 by Sir John Talbot and died there of the plague towards the close of the same year.[11] Felim's son, John, lived at Ross Castle, an O'Reilly stronghold on Loch Sheelin, from which he was evicted by the English. He then went to live at Kilskeir where his grandson, John, married Elizabeth, daughter of Thomas Plunkett of Crosskeel, County Meath, with whom he got the estate of Ballinlough, then called Lough-Bomoyle. A descendant, James O'Reilly, married Barbara, the daughter of Andrew Nugent of Tullaghan; she was the maternal granddaughter of Thomas Nugent, 4th Earl of Westmeath.

James and Barbara had three sons: Hugh, Andrew, and James. Hugh, who was born in 1741, married, in 1781, Catherine Mary Anne, daughter of Charles Matthew of Annefield, and niece of the first Earl of LLandaff. Hugh was created a Baronet in 1795 and in 1812, being left an estate by Governor Nugent, his maternal uncle, he was obliged to take the name and arms of Nugent. He died in 1821. His younger brother, Andrew, born in 1742, had a distinguished career in the Austrian army; he served under the Archduke Maximilian and when the latter abandoned Vienna, Count Andrew was appointed Governor. While serving in the Austrian army he achieved a certain notoriety by fighting a duel with a Major Count Kleberg over a rich heiress who showed a preference for O'Reilly. He left his opponent dead, after a battle which lasted two hours and fifty minutes. He was afterwards court-martialed but was acquitted. He married the heiress, Maria Barbara, Countess of Sweerts and Spork, in 1784. Having no children of his own he adopted the son of his brother Hugh, as his heir. Napoleon referred to him as *"le respectable General O'Reilly."* He died in Vienna on July 3rd, 1882, aged 90.

Sir Hugh Nugent died in 1821 leaving two sons, James who succeeded as 2nd Baronet, and John. In 1811 Sir James married Susanne, daughter of Baron D'Arabet, but died without issue in 1843. John, born in 1800, entered the Austrian service; he was adopted by his uncle Count Andrew and resumed his original surname of O'Reilly. In 1842 he returned to Ireland and married Letitia Maria, daughter of Charles White Roche of Ballyran County Limerick. On the death of his brother he succeeded to the baronetcy and all the family estates, and reluctantly, resumed the name of Nugent. He died in February 1859 and was succeeded by his eldest son, born in 1845.[12]

Count Andrew O'Reilly was a Knight Commander of the Order of Maria Teresa. He distinguished himself at the battles of Montebello, Marengo, and Austerlitz. His younger brother, James who was also in the Austrian service, was killed in the Turkish war of 1788.[13]

Some Other O'Reillys

Throughout the long period of their history the O'Reillys have given many priests and prelates to the

Church; five O'Reillys have held the Primacy of Armagh. Five were bishops of Kilmore, two of Clogher, and one of Derry.

Of all these surely the most outstanding was Hugh O'Reilly, bishop of Kilmore and later, Primate of Armagh. He was born in the year 1580 or 1581, probaly at Ballintemple in the barony of Clanmahon[14] where his father Maolmordha had an estate. Maolmordha was the son of Aodh, son of Fergal, son of Sean, son of Cathal.[15] Hugh was thus a direct descendant of Giolla Iosa Ruadh and a member of the ruling family of Breifne. He received his education at the Franciscan monastery of Cavan and this probably strongly influenced him towards the priesthood. There is some doubt as to the date of his ordination but it is known that he studied philosophy at Rouen in 1618 and also studied theology at Paris; so it is pretty certain that he was ordained before that date. O'Connell states[16] that he was ordained in 1618 but this seems highly improbable as he would then have been about 35 years of age. In 1625 he was appointed to the bishopric of Kilmore by Pope Urban VIII and was consecrated in St. Peter's Church, Droghedha in July 1626 by Dr. Thomas Fleming, Archbishop of Dublin.

Hugh O'Reilly inherited a troubled domain in Kilmore. At the time of his birth the O'Reillys were still strong in Breifne, where another Maolmordha (Chief of Breifne from 1535 to 1565) had put up a stout resistance to the incursions of the English. By the time he was appointed to Kilmore, the Plantation had taken place, and his family had been deprived of their estates in Ballintemple and been given a miserable 300 acres in the barren and desolate barony of Tullyhaw. Moreover, there was strong persecution of the Catholics in an endeavour to induce them to conform to the established church: "The see had been vacant for nearly twenty years, the native power was broken, and the chieftains either mur-

Seal Matrix of Bishop Hugh O'Reilly (1580–1652?), Bishop of Kilmore and later Primate of Armagh.

dered or exiled, the churches confiscated, and the land-owners dispossessed."[17]

Not long after Hugh's appointment two of the most vicious of the Lords Justices arrived in Cavan, bent on enforcing the penal laws against Catholics and of forcing them to attend Protestant worship. It will be recalled that by this time the Cathedral of Kilmore and the Bishop's residence were in Protestant hands.

These two ruffians, Boyle, Earl of Cork, and Viscount Ely, set out to encompass the arrest of Bishop O'Reilly but this they failed to do owing to the help given him by the peasantry who kept him hidden until these two departed from Breifne.

Despite these hardships, Bishop O'Reilly set about reorganising the diocese, establishing places for the celebration of Mass and regular administration of the Sacraments. The Sacrament of Confirmation particularly, had been neglected and the Bishop himself records that at one time he confirmed no less than fifteen hundred persons a day, throughout a period of three weeks. He also found considerable laxity amongst the clergy, particularly in the matter of dress, abuse of alcohol, and concubinage. These matters he dealt with rigorously, even to the extent of depriving several priests of their offices and exercising a direct control over the admission of individuals to ordination.

In 1626 the Primatial See of Armagh became vacant and Bishop O'Reilly's name was one of those put forward. Although he was not chosen on that occasion it is of interest to note what was said of him by the Earls of Tyrone and Tyrconnell on whose lists he appeared in second place. "He is a native of Ulster, a member of one of the leading Irish families; he now dwells in Ireland and is Bishop of Kilmore. He is of mature age, of blameless life, well-versed in both laws, and also in sacred theology, and is very acceptable to the clergy, nobles and people of Armagh."[18] However, he was appointed to the See in 1628 and took up his duties in 1630 on receiving the pallium from Rome.

In the Primacy he was faced by very much the same problems as he had encountered in Kilmore and he dealt with them in the same rigorous but understanding fashion. One of his first acts was to establish regular provincial synods for the discussion and settlement of problems of ecclesiastical administration and discipline. The first of these was held in the diocese of Ardagh in 1632, and a second was held in 1637, at both of which O'Reilly presided. For some reason the authorities suspected that the 1637 synod was a cover for some kind of subversive activity; the Archbishop was arrested and confined to prison for six months until they became convinced of his innocence.

The next synod was held at Kells in 1642 and it was here that the foundations of the Confederation of Kilkenny were laid. Owing to the disturbed state of the country and the continuing hostility of the authorities to the Catholic Hierarchy, the Archbishop lived most of the time in the houses of his relatives in Kilmore and it was here that he was visited, in 1646, by Monsignor Massari, Dean of Fermo and secretary to the Papal Nuncio, Rinucinni. Massari gives the following account of his interview with the Archbishop in Loch Uachtair Castle:

The Archbishop of Armagh, Primate of Ireland, arrived to visit me. He is a man of noble birth, great influence, prudence, learning, goodness, noble heart, is worthy of the highest esteem, and is most devoted to the Holy Apostolic See and to the Supreme Pontiff. I detained him for dinner and after a stay of many hours with me, he returned to his temporary residence not far away, leaving me with a high idea and an extraordinary impression of his worth, wisdom, and learning. The good prelate was particularly anxious that while the glow of victory was still fresh a march should be made on Dublin to smash the Marquis of Ormond, for, said he, that venomous serpent must be struck on the head, and were the city once captured we would be delivered from the perfidious artifices and iniquitous wiles of an adversary who is no Irishman but rather an enemy to his country. [19]

On November 6th 1649 the great Confederate leader, Owen Roe O'Neill died in Loch Uachtair Castle. A few days later he was interred in the Franciscan Monastery of Cavan where the Primate, in the presence of a great concourse of clergy and laity, officiated at the graveside. Not long afterwards the Primate himself who was in failing health retired to the Priory of Holy Trinity in Loch Uachtair and there, on July 29th 1651 he presided over his last synod which was concerned with matters of ecclesiastical administration and with measures for resisting the Puritan regime.

There is some doubt as to the actual date of the Primate's death. Renahan[20] gives it as July 7th 1651. A manuscript in the Royal Irish Academy gives it as 1653: *Aodh O Raghallaigh Priomfaidh na hEireann do dol deg 1653*.[21] Cardinal Moran gave the date as February 1653 but later changed this to 1652. O'Connell[22] says there is no evidence that the Primate was living in 1653 and that he seems to have died towards the end of 1652.

The body of the Primate was conveyed to the Franciscan monastery of Cavan where it was interred with his ancestors; according to popular tradition he was buried in the choir of the ruined church, long since uprooted and desecrated. "It was a holy thought to lay the bones of so true a prelate in the same loam with the chieftains of his own race and kindred."[23] The Primate's chalice, made of silver is now preserved in Cavan Cathedral. It bears the following inscription:

Hugo Reilly Kilmorensis Eps. in honorem pretiosi sanguinis Xti. me fieri fecit 1628.

As a patron of learning Primate O'Reilly occupies an honoured place in the history of his time. It was at his suggestion and encouraged by his help and patronage that Father Colgan, the Irish Franciscan historian compiled his monumental work, *Acta Sanctorum Hiberniae*. In his preface to the work, which is dedicated to Primate O'Reilly, Father Colgan acknowledges his obligations to the archbishop, "who cheered him on in his undertakings, and secured for him the sympathy and aid of his suffragans." Father Colgan and his community were unable to undertake the publication of such a voluminous work, but the Primate, out of his scanty revenues, advanced the money for its publication. The *Acta Sanctorum Hiberniae* is the greatest work on Irish hagiology which has ever appeared. It is a monument to the industry of the Irish Franciscans of Louvain and remains an eloquent testimony to the generosity and patronage of Primate O'Reilly who, in a merciless age, when terrorism and persecution reigned supreme in Ireland, contrived to help and encourage them in their great work.[24]

Hugh O'Reilly's kinsman, Edmund O'Reilly, succeeded him as Primate of Armagh. He was born in 1606 and was ordained in 1629. After ordination he spent some time studying at the University of Louvain. He returned to Dublin in 1642 and was appointed Vicar-General of the diocese but was arrested in 1653 and transported to the continent. On his appointment to the Primatial See he was consecrated at Brussels but in the following year, on attempting to return to Ireland, he was arrested when passing through London and sent back to France. A year later he succeeded in entering Ireland, heavily disguised, and remained there for about two years, but was again driven out in 1661. He again returned to Ireland in 1666 and remained hidden in Dublin for less than a month, when he was again discovered and transported to the continent. He never returned, and died in March 1669 at the Royal College of Saumur in France.[25]

Another O'Reilly who occupied the Primatial See was Dr. Michael O'Reilly who was Vicar-General of Kilmore under the administration of Primate Hugh MacMahon from 1714 to 1730. He studied in Rome, where he was ordained, having obtained doctorates in Theology, Canon Law, and Civil Law. He was a close friend and confidant of the great Primate MacMahon who thought very highly of him. In 1739 Dr. O'Reilly was appointed bishop of Derry which he administered under the most difficult circumstances; there were no churches, nothing more than hovels or sheltered rocks for the celebration of mass, and the ignorance of their religion by the people, after long years of repression, was such that Dr. O'Reilly compiled two catechisms for their instruction, one in Irish and the other in English, which were so highly appreciated that they remained in use until quite recent times.

In January 1749 Pope Benedict XIV promoted Bishop O'Reilly to the Primatial See of Armagh, where he remained until his death in 1758.

Daniel O'Reilly who was born about the year 1700 in the townland of Drumgora in the district of Lurgan, studied at Douai in France and afterwards in the Irish College at Antwerp, of which he ultimately became president. From there he was appointed bishop of Clogher in 1747. After his death in 1778 he was succeeded in the bishopric by his nephew Hugh O'Reilly who ruled there until 1801.

In the parish of Drumgoon near Cootehill there was an important branch of the O'Reillys who gave many priests to the church. The principal seat of this family was in the townland of Crann in Drumgoon parish, hence the ecclesiastical members of the family were popularly known as the Crann O'Reillys; one of them was Charles O'Reilly bishop of Kilmore who was born in 1750. His father's name was Owen and his mother's maiden name was Brady; she came from Kildrumsheridan. The bishop was educated abroad, and on his return to Ireland was a curate for some years in his own parish of Drumgoon. In 1793 he was appointed co-adjutor to Dr. Maguire and on the death of the latter, in 1798, succeeded him as bishop. He was the first bishop of Kilmore since the early sixteenth century to have a settled home in the diocese. Unfortunately, his episcopacy was a brief one; he died at Cootehill on March 5th 1800 and was buried, at his own request, with his relatives in the old cemetery of Kildrumsheridan. His tomb is covered by a massive slab which displays the O'Reilly coat of arms and bears the following inscription:

Hoc monumentum erectus fuit in memoriam illustrissimi D.D. Caroli O'Reilly episcopi catholici Kilmorensis qui in domino obdormivit die quinto martii 1800 anno aetatis quinquagesimo. Requiscat in pace.

Another of the Crann O'Reillys was the Rev. Farrell O'Reilly, P.P. of Drumlane who was appointed bishop of Kilmore in 1806. He was the son of Terence and Honora O'Reilly (nee Clark) and was born about 1741. He was a native of the parish of Moybolge, to which his ancestors had moved from the townland of Crann. His father was one of the seven sons of John O'Reilly of Drummore in Killann parish. There is a detailed account of the family in *Breifne* Vol II. No. 6. (1963) by Philip O'Connell in which he suggests that John O'Reilly is identical with the Sean son of Maolmordha, son of Philip, mentioned in the *O'Reilly Pedigree* 15. (2). The bishop studied on the continent, probably at Louvain; he was ordained about 1766 and on his return to Kilmore was eventually appointed P.P. of Drumlane where he remained until his elevation to the bishopric. In his later years he became somewhat frail and died at Baileboro while on visitation, on April 30th 1829, being then 88 years old.

At Lismullig, Poles, near Cavan town there is a family of O'Reillys whose ancestors are said to have been evicted from Tonogh, Mount Nugent, some 300 years ago. One of the earlier members of the family was Fr. Patrick John O'Reilly who was a priest in the diocese of Bordeaux. He was born at Poles in 1806 and studied for the priesthood in France. In 1860 he published a work in three volumes entitled *Histoire Complete de Bordeaux*. He was an outstanding man in the world of French literature and a member of many literary Societes. Among his works were, *Histoire de Verdelais* (1840), and *Essai sur La Ville de Bazas* (1840).

Fr. O'Reilly was the Cure of Montferrand. He died at the Hospital of St. Andre of Bordeaux on January 28th 1861; there is a memorial to him in the town. Three further volumes of the *Histoire Compléte de Bordeaux* were published posthumously in 1863.[26]

Any history of the O'Reillys must include John Boyle O'Reilly, Irish revolutionary and author. He was born on June 28th 1844 at Dowth Castle on the Boyne, four miles from Drogheda and was the son of William Boyle O'Reilly who, for 35 years, was the master of the National school attached to the Netterville Institution for widows and orphans at Dowth Castle. His mother was Elizabeth Boyle, the daughter of a Dublin tradesman.

He was arrested at Islandbridge barracks on February 13th 1866, on a charge that having come to the knowledge of an internal mutiny in H.M. forces in Ireland, he failed to give information about this to his commanding officer; he was a trooper in the 10th Hussars, having enlisted as an agent of the Irish Republican Brotherhood for the purpose of securing the adhesion of Irish soldiers to the revolutionary movement.

After a twelve-day trial he was convicted and sentenced to be shot but the sentence was commuted to twenty years penal servitude. He was eventually transported to a convict settlement in Australia, but managed to escape in April 1869. He settled in Boston as a journalist and became editor and part proprietor of *The Pilot* published in that town; he became one of the most influential R.C. Irish American publishers in the United States.[27] His epitaph in Boston was thus written: "Ireland gave him birth, England gave him exile, America gave him fame."

William O'Reilly of Kilnacrott was a prominent figure in Cavan political and religious affairs from 1824 to

1831. In 1826 he took part in a controversy regarding the make up of the poll for the barony of Tullyhaw. Apparently he lived in Mountjoy Square, Dublin, but was often designated William O'Reilly of Kilnacrott. Rev. P. Cunningham states "I have been unable to trace such a person at this period; it may be that he was the William O'Reilly (1792-1844) second son of Matthew O'Reilly of Thomastown Castle County Meath, who was descended from Edmond of Kilnacrott."[28] This William O'Reilly was one of the first members of the Catholic Association and achieved some notoriety by his attempt to block the appointment of Eneas Mc Donnell as the Association's London representative in 1824. His son, Myles O'Reilly, commanded the Irish Brigade in the Papal Army in 1860.

Hugh Reilly, born in Cavan, was Master in Chancery and Clerk of the Council in Ireland during the reign of James II who appointed him Lord Chancellor of Ireland Later he was dismissed by the king because of a book written by him: "Ireland's Case Briefly Stated," giving an account of the misfortunes suffered by Catholics from the time of Elizabeth to that of James himself. The date of his birth is unknown but he died about 1695.

Though not a native of Breifne proper, Thomas Devin Reilly, son of a solicitor, born in Monaghan in 1824, was one of the most outspoken and fearless revolutionary writers of his time. He was a frequent contributor to the *Nation* and later to *The United Irishman*, though his fiery temper, his impetuosity, and his propensity for taking instant dislikes made him a difficult colleague. Indeed the only person with whom he formed a lasting friendship was Mitchell, and after the latter's trial and conviction he deemed it prudent to leave Ireland. He fled to New York where he ultimately became editor of the *Democratic Review*. He died suddenly in Washington in 1854 and was buried in Mount Olivet cemetery where a monument to his memory was erected by his fellow countrymen in exile. Mitchell wrote of him as "the largest heart, the most enduring spirit, the loftiest genius of all Irish rebels who, in all the wild activity of his life, never aimed low and never spoke falsely."

Another O'Reilly born outside the confines of Breifne proper was Edward O'Reilly the distinguished lexicographer, who compiled an Irish-English dictionary. He was assistant secretary to the Iberno Celtic Society and in 1824 received an award from the Royal Irish Academy for his essay on the Brehon Laws; he gained another in 1829 for an essay on the poems of Ossian. His death took place in August 1829.

The O'Reilly Money

According to John O'Donovan[29] the O'Reillys coined their own money at Crossakeel near Kells, County Meath. Alice Stopford Green in her book *The Making of Ireland and Its Undoing* gives a lyrical description of commercial activities in Breifne:

In Cavan, lying in the shelter of the morasses and mazes of Lough Oughter we may still trace the remains of a peaceful and undefended trading centre . . . the sunny valley with gardens stretching up the hills, the great monastery, and by its side on a low lift of grass, the palace and business centre of the O'Reillys, among the greatest of trading chiefs whose money was spread by their traffic all over Ireland and was even commonly current in England.

I have been unable to find anything in the historical references to Breifne which would support this rosy picture; it reads suspiciously like a view seen through a Celtic mist.

In 1447 an Anglo-Irish parliament met at Trim and passed the following legislation:

". . . Forasmuch as the clipping of the coin of our lord the King has caused divers men in this land of Ireland to counterfeit the said coin . . . wherefore it is ordained and agreed by

147

authority of this present parliament that no money so clipped
be received in any place in the said land, from the first day of
May next to come, nor the money of Oraylly or any other un-
lawful money . . . .

Again, in 1456, a similar parliament met at Naas
and recorded the fact that "the Irish silver called Reilly's
increase from one day to another, to the great injury
and impoverishment of his said people of this his said
land and annihilation of his said land. . . ."
Documentary evidence, including the above statutes
were collected and published by Dom Nolan O.S,B. in
two volumes entitled *The Monetary History of Ireland* in
1926. Based on this evidence Mr. M.W. O'Reilly stated:

We are thus left in no doubt that the O'Reilly money circu-
lated freely in the fifteenth century and perhaps for a hundred
years before, not alone in the great areas under independent
Irish rule, but in the smaller part then ruled by the English.
There are certain silver farthings known to numismatists
which Lindsay[30] has pronounced to be probably from the
mints of Irish princes in the fourteenth and fifteenth centuries, but some may be of the twelfth century or even
earlier.[31]

O'Reilly draws an interesting comparison between
certain of these early coins and the seal of Sir John
O'Reilly: "The designs on the seal are unquestionably of
the petroglyph or primographic type. Their presence on this
sixteenth-century seal is extraordinary and is an example,
which sometimes occurs in this country, of the survival
of an old custom over many centuries. The wheel like
figures on the seal closely resemble some of the wheel
oghams on Stone O O. Cairn T. Loughcrew, Oldcastle,
County Meath which borders the O'Reilly country, but
the Loughcrew ciphers may be dated about 500 B.C. It
might be conjectured that the ciphers on the seal represent wheel oghams which once appeared on the pillar

Seal Matrix of Sir John O'Reilly. The inscription reads IOHA DUKES ORELI MILES, which translates "Seal of John, Leader of Reillys."

stones which still stand at the place of inauguration of the Kings of Brefney and Lords and Chiefs of the O'Reillys at Shantemon. These, and most other places of inauguration were taken over from the pagans as Tara itself was, where the Kings of All Ireland were inaugurated. It can be shown that such symbols and ciphers have an hieratic or sacred character, and their presence on this seal attests the religious and literary culture of the O'Reillys even in the hour of decay."

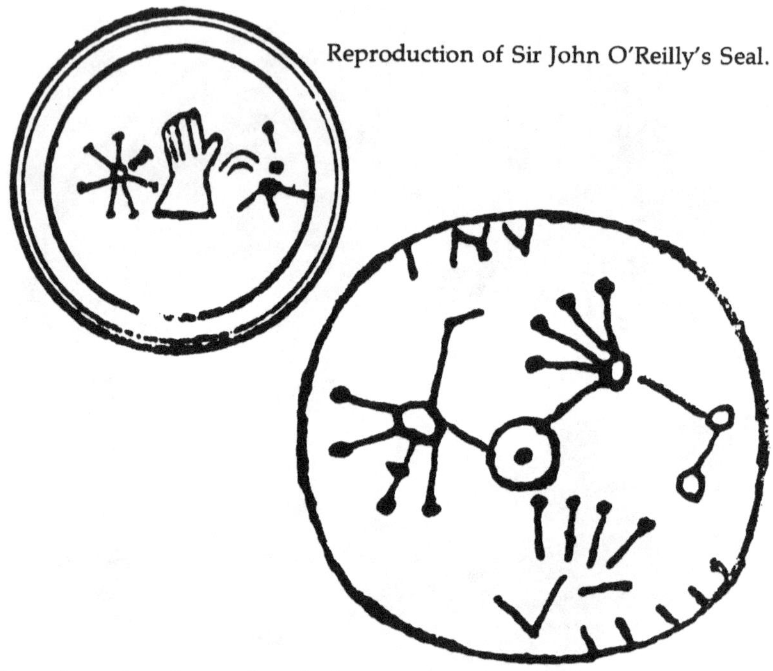

Drawing of a silver coin which may or may not be an O'Reilly coin. The markings tend to follow those on Sir John O'Reilly's seal, thus adding weight to its being an O'Reilly coin.

In support of his argument the author reproduces a silver coin (shown above) bought in England. "It has no provenance, but for the reasons given above it is pronounced to be Irish and as the rayed circles resemble the ciphers on Sir John's seal, it may be one of the famous 'O'Reillys'. The ogham system of writing was never forgotten in Ireland, and if the O'Reilly used it on his seal his moneyer might well have used it on the coinage. There remains the difficulty that these 'O'Reillys' and other Irish coins have never been found to bear a literary inscription. This, of course, makes their identification very difficult. However, that some of these coins are the veritable 'O'Reillys' of history is amply proved by two facts: firstly, that the O'Reillys only, of all the Irish clans, are on record as having coined money, and, secondly, that some of the coins in question bear primograph ciphers like those on Sir John O'Reilly's seal, while the Hand symbol, so prominent there is also found, though rarely, on these Irish coins."

I am indebted to this author for the elucidation of the inscription on Sir John's seal:

IOHA DUKES ORELI MILES

This is a contraction for "Sigillum Johannes Duces O Reli Miles," i.e. "The Seal of John, Leader (or Duke) of the O'Reillys. Knight." As the S of Miles is of necessity beside the I or J of John on the round seal; the S stands for, by a synaresis, the last letter of the first, and the initial of the second, word.

Despite the plausible case made out above, no coins have ever been found which can be identified as genuine O'Reilly money. Michael Dolley and W.A. Seaby have pointed out[32] that the clipping of English coin was extensively practiced in Ireland about the middle of the fifteenth century and this has been confirmed by the finding of hoards of clipped coins of the period Edward III to Henry VI. In April 1852 there was found at Pettigo in County Fermanagh, a most interesting group of forgeries of unclipped Scottish groats, produced by hammering thin sheets of silver over actual coins and then pairing up the resultant cliches with a lead solder core.

Dolley and Seaby state that an examination of two so called "O'Reillys" in the Ulster Museum showed that they were made by cementing with a lead solder foil impressions of both sides of clipped genuine coins. In their opinion these coins are imitations of clipped En-

O'Reilly's money (Ulster Museum) (reverses and obverses). These coins were probably all cut down to the required size for use in Ireland during the 15th century.

(1) Edward III. Groat, pre-treaty issue, London (1351–61) cut to size of penny.

(2) Ditto.

(3) Edward III. Half Groat, Treaty issue, London (1362–69). cut to size of penny.

(4) Edward III. Half Groat, Post-Treaty issue, or Richard II. early issue, London. (1370–90). cut to size of penny.

(5) Henry V. Groat of London (1413–22), cut to size of penny.

(6) Henry VI. Groat of Calais, annulet issue (1422–47), cut to size of penny. This example consists of two silver clichés (this consists of sheets of silver hammered over genuine coin) united by lead silver core.

(7) Henry VI. Groat of Calais, annulet issue (1422–27), cut to size of Half Groat.

(8) Ditto.

(9) Henry VI. Groat of Calais, annulet issue, (1422–27), cut to size of penny.

(10) Henry VI. Half-Groat of Calais, pine-cone-mascle issue, (1430–34), cut to size of penny.

(11) Edward IV. Anglo-Irish Groat of Dublin, English type, light issue (1473–78) with annulet either side of neck, Rosettes in 2nd and 4th angles. Cut to size of Irish Half Groat.

(12) Edward IV. Anglo-Irish Groat of Dublin. Similar to No. 11. but with rosettes in 1st and 3rd angles. Cut to size of Irish Half-Groat.

(For further details see Dolley and Seaby in B.N.J. XXXVI (1967), pp.114–117.)

List of Co. Cavan 17th Century Penny Tokens.

(1) *Ballyjamesduff. Obv.* JOHN·DALIN·1668 = I.E.D. *Rev.* BAL-LYIAMES·DVFFE = the Mercer's Arms; a maidenhead. Williamson 61. Example in National Museum of Ireland, Dublin (probably Aquilla Smith Coll.).

(2) *Cavan. Obv.* ·IOHN·BOLLARD = shield of arms; six rondels 3, 2 and 1, in chief demi-lion rampant, I·M·E in field. *Rev.* IN·CA-VAN·1673 = a swan hissing (in reeds on nest). Large size. Williamson. Example in Ulster Museum, Belfast (T.S. Agnew Coll.).

(3) *Cavan. Obv.* IOHN·BALLARD = a swan hissing (on nest). *Rev.* ·IN·CAVAN·1667 = I.M.B. Small size. Williamson 159. Example in British Museum (Fletcher Collection).

(4) *Belturbet. Obv.* ROBART·IIARES·AT = a pair of shears and a curry comb. *Rev.* BELLTVRBEATT DYER = 1d. (between mullets). Williamson 112 (variety). Example in National Museum of Ireland, Dublin.

(5) *Killashandra. Obv.* LAMES·FORREST·MARCHANT = a castle (with 3 towers). *Rev.* IN·KILLYSHANDRI·1667 = merchant's mark and anchor combined between I F. Williamson 534. Example in British Museum (Fletcher Coll.).

(6) *Belturbet. Obv.* RICHARD·HARRISON· = postman on horse-back carrying bugle horn. *Rev.* BELTVRBAT·POSTMR· = D I between lozenges. Williamson 113. Example in National Museum of Ire-land, Dublin (Aquilla Smith Coll.).

glish groats of Henry VI and Edward IV and were made about the years 1445-1455 in O'Reilly's country of Breifne. "Let us hope," they said, "that the Chief himself had nothing to do with them for they were really counterfeit coins." Mr. W.A. Seaby, Senior Research Assistant in the Numismatics Department of the Ulster Museum, has kindly supplied me with photographs of these coins, which are reproduced in this text.

Trade tokens were in use in Ulster, possibly from at least the twelfth century; it was however, during the seventeenth and eighteenth centuries that token coins enjoyed a general circulation. In those days there was a scarcity of small change and the government at times, allowed traders to issue their own coins, usually copper penny tokens. The issuers were responsible for the tokens and were obliged to provide goods or ordinary currency in exchange when requested to do so.

It is known that token coins bearing the names of traders in Cavan, Belturbet, Ballyjamesduff, and Killeshandra were once in circulation. I am again indebted to Mr. Seaby for photographs of these tokens; the source of each example is acknowledged in the descriptive notes accompanying the photographs. The swan on the Ballard coin is said to represent the sign of a very old house, No. 63 Main Street, which was burnt down with a number of others in 1880. In the list of Cavan burgesses is found the name of John Ballard who took the oath of office on August 31st 1704.

The Royal Mint again issued Irish copper money in the eighteenth century but private tokens were in use in places in the following century until about 1860. Finally all token coins were declared illegal by Act of Parliament.

The O'Reilly Coat of Arms

The O'Reilly Coat of Arms is set out on page 22 of the Annals of the Kingdom of Ireland as follows:

Arms

Two lions supporting a dexter hand proper.

Crest

An oak tree on a mount with a snake
descending its trunk proper.

Motto

Fortitudine et Prudentia.

The Right Hand is the principal symbol of the
O'Reillys. It represents the *Dextra Dei* or Right Hand of
God the Father raised in benediction. The lion rampant
is very common in Irish heraldry, symbolising the war-
rior head of the clan or sept, while the tree represents
the tree of life and by analogy, the Tree of the Cross.
The serpent also appears with great frequency on Irish
Coats of Arms, and is said to stem from a tradition that
Milesius, the reputed ancestor of the O'Reillys and other
princely families, carried this symbol on his standard to
commemorate the miraculous recovery of his nephew
Gaodhal from a snake bite.

The Hand symbol has been known from very early
times, and according to M.W. O'Reilly[33] is found on the
standard of the Red Branch Knights. The author, who
claimed to have discovered no less than seventeen different O'Reilly Coats of Arms, has an interesting reference
to an ancient bronze plaque, now in the library of Trinity College, which he believes is the earliest known
example of the O'Reilly Arms, dating from the 12th or
13th century. The plaque shows a cross "raguley" (i.e.
"with the bark and the stumps of branches on it") with
arms upraised and two animals snarling at each other on
either side of an upraised hand mounted on what appears to be a bishop's mitre. The animals certainly do
not represent lions, and on the whole the evidence for

its being an O'Reilly Coat of Arms is unconvincing.

The earliest authentic example of the O'Reilly Hand occurs on the seal of Sir John O'Reilly (1583-1596) where it appears alone. On the Plunkett-O'Reilly tombstone in Clonabreaney churchyard, County Meath, bearing the date 1581 there appears the first example of the Coat of Arms, showing two lions supporting a dexter hand. The seal of Primate Hugh O'Reilly (1628-1653) shows an oak tree between a lion rampant and a dexter hand couped at the wrist.

The next coat of arms in order of date is found on a tombstone in Tallaght churchyard, County Dublin. It shows two lions rampant combatant, supporting a dexter hand and an oak tree rising out of a ducal coronet. The tomb is that of Nicholas Really and the stone records that it was erected by his son Barnaby Really, gentleman, in 1677. There is a similar coat of arms in Ballymachus churchyard on the northern shore of Loch Sheelin; here the crest is a helmet and the date is 1720.

On the smaller of the two O'Reilly mausoleums in Kildrumfertan churchyard there is a coat of arms showing two lions rampant combatant supporting a dexter hand, with the motto *Dum Spiro Spero;* no such motto is attributed to the O'Reilly family in any treatise on heraldry. On the larger mausoleum there is another coat of arms showing the two lions rampant combatant but supporting a hand sinister couped at the wrist, with a crest depicting an oak tree rising out of a ducal coronet, a serpent descending the trunk; the motto is *Fortitudine et Prudentia.* Except for the hand sinister this is the conventional Coat of Arms of the Clan. The ducal coronet has reference to the earlier designation of the head of the O'Reillys as Duke of Breifne.

M.W. O'Reilly states that during the early part of the eighteenth century a curious change occurred; the hand begins to be portrayed as bleeding. He points out that at this time the fortunes of the family had reached a low ebb and some of its members had "verted to Protestantism." He attributes a spiritual significance to this change, which he avers occurred in other ages and countries at times of national disaster. He describes two examples of this new coat of arms, which he states were granted by the Ulster King-at-Arms, the only authority on heraldry until 1943 when this office was transferred to Eire. The first example is the coat of arms of William Joseph O'Reilly Esq. of Knock Abbey, County Louth, Private Chamberlain to the Pope. It shows a quartered shield with, in two quarters the two lions rampant combatant supporting a dexter hand couped at the wrist and bleeding, whilst in one of the remaining quarters there is an oak tree with serpent entwined, and, in the other, three discs, which he suggests symbolise the Sacred Host. The second example is the coat of arms of Myles George O'Reilly of Heath House, County Leitrim which displays in two quarters the Divine Hand, again with drops of blood, and, in the other two quarters, the tree and serpent.

There was, however, an earlier development in heraldry which may have had some bearing on the above mentioned changes. Following the Plantation of Ulster in 1609 baronetcies were awarded to certain of the English settlers with a grant of arms which showed a left hand with three drops of blood falling from the wrist. This device is said to have been derived from the legend concerning two warriors crossing the channel to Ulster who made a pact with each other that the first to land on its soil should be its sole possessor; the one who was lagging behind cut off his left hand and hurled it onto the beach in front of his rival.

MacLysaght[34] gives the O'Reilly Coat of Arms as: "Vert two lions rampant, combatant or supporting a dexter hand couped at the wrist erect and apaumée bloody proper." It is a remarkable fact that of twenty Irish families shown in MacLysaght as having the hand in their coats of arms the only one showing the hand bleeding is that of the O'Reillys. Can it be that some of the clan received this "bloody hand" as a reward for their loyalty to the English?

Notes

1. *The Irish Brigades*. Vol. I. p 274.
2. B.A.S. Jn. Vol II. No. 1. 1923.
3. *Gen. Hist.* (11) 3.
4. Op. cit.
5. *Burke's Landed Gentry.*
6. Op. cit.
7. Op. cit.
8. *Gen. Hist.* (11) 3.
9. "The Last Colonel of the Irish Brigade". Mrs Morgan John O'Connell. Vol. I. p 303.
10. *Irish Book Lover.* Vol. 22. 1934.
11. *Kilmore.* (footnote. p 305).
12. Duffy. *The O'Reillys of the Present Time.* Feb. 1861. O'Donovan.
13. *The Irish Brigades.* Vol I. p 276. J.C. O'Callaghan.
14. "Rev. Hugh O'Reilly, a Reforming Primate." *Breifne* Vol IV. No. 13. 1970. Seamus P. O'Mordha. M.A.
15. *Gen. Hist.* p 88 (17).
16. *Kilmore.* p 405.
17. Op. cit. p 394.
18. *Breifne.* Vol. IV. No. 13. 1970. Seamus P. O'mordha. M.A.
19. *The Catholic Bulletin.* Dublin. 1917.
20. *Collections of Irish History.* E.IV. Fol. 51,52. Renahan.
21. Op. cit.
22. *Kilmore.* p 420.
23. *Irish Franciscan Monasteries.* 5th Edition. p 183. Rev. C.P. Meehan.
24. *Kilmore.* p 421.
25. Op. cit. p 434 (footnote).
26. O'Connell. Private communication.
27. *John Boyle O'Reilly. His Life, Poems & Speeches.* James Jeffrey Roche.
28. *Breifne.* 1962. p 42. Revd. P. Cunningham.
29. Duffy. February 1861.
30. *The O'Reillys of Templemills, Celbridge. 1941.* By M.W. O'Reilly Esq. F.C.I.I.; Moorfield Dundrum Co. Dublin.

31. View of the Coinage of Ireland. p 24.

32. "Le Money Del O'Rayley". (O'Reilly's Money). B.N.J. Vol. XXXVI. 1964. Michael Dolley & W.A. Seaby.

33. *The O'Reillys of Templemills.*

34. *Irish Families. Their Names, Arms, and Origins.* Edward Mac-Lysaght. Dublin. Allen Figgis ' Co. Ltd. 1957.

CHAPTER VIII

Other Breifne Families

The Nugents

Although the Nugents were not an indigenous Irish family, their long and intimate, if not always harmonious, relationship with the O'Reillys justifies a detailed description of them.

The family is descended from Nogent de Retrou of the illustrious house of Bellesme in Normandy. Two brothers of the family, Gilbert and Hugh, accompanied William the Conqueror from Normandy and were with him at the battle of Hastings. In the reign of Henry II in the year 1172, Sir Gilbert de Nogent, with his brothers, Richard, Christopher, and John, came in the expedition to Ireland in company with Sir Hugh de Lacy. Sir Gilbert married the sister of de Lacy and obtained with her the barony of Delvin in County Westmeath.

Delvin was so called after the druid Delbaeth of the Dalcassian race of Thomond; having been driven from his territory in Clare he travelled north and one of his sons settled in the eastern part of Westmeath, afterwards known as Dealbhna. After the Norman invasion the territory passed into the hands of de Lacy. The castle erected by Sir Gilbert de Nogent can still be seen in the main street of Delvin.

Sir Gilbert died in 1202 without issue; he was succeeded by his brother, Richard. Richard's only duaghter and heiress married Richard le Tuit and carried the barony of Delvin into the family of John (or James) Tuite, where it remained until brought back by the marriage of Sir William Nugent of Balrath who was descended from Christopher Nugent's third son to Catherine, daughter and heiress of John Fitzjames, Baron Delvin.

Christopher, 11th Baron, married Elizabeth Preston, daughter of Sir Robert Preston, first Viscount Gormanstown. Their son Richard was born in 1462 and succeeded as 12th baron in 1483. He was summoned to parliament in 1486, 1490, and 1491, and was appointed leader in chief of all forces destined for the defence of Dublin, Meath, Louth, and Kildare. In 1494 Garret Mór, Earl of Kildare, gave his niece in marriage to Richard and in the following year a son, Christopher, was born.

In 1504 Garret Mór set out on a punitive expedition against his son-in-law Ulick McWilliam Burke of Clanrickard who had so ill-treated his wife that she was forced to leave him. On this expedition Garret Mór was accompanied by the Baron of Delvin and also by O'Reilly of Breifne, amongst others. This O'Reilly presumably would be John son of Cathal, son of Eoghan na Feisoge, who was chief from 1491 to 1510. A fierce battle took place at Knock Tuagh (i.e. the Hill of the Axes) so called because of the enormous numbers of gallowglasses who were slaughtered there. Indeed so fierce was the battle that the site was afterwards called Ballybrone (The Place of Sorrow).

In 1513 Garret Mór died; in 1514 his son, Garret Óge led an expedition into Breifne, burned the castle of Tullymongan to the ground and slew the chief, Hugh, the brother and successor of John O'Reilly. This was in retaliation for a raid which O'Reilly and O'More had made into the Pale. In the raid on Cavan town Philip, the brother of Hugh, Philip's son, together with some fourteen of the leading O'Reillys and large numbers of their followers were also slain.

In 1520 Garret Óge married Lady Elizabeth Grey, daughter of the Marquis of Dorset and sister of the ill-fated Lady Jane. They had three children: Elizabeth ("the Fair Geraldine") and two sons, Gerald and Edward. Gerald became 11th Earl of Kildare and his daughter, Mary, married married Christopher, Baron Delvin. Edward's son, Gerald became 14th Earl of Kildare and is said to have married Lady Elizabeth Nugent, daughter of the 14th Baron Delvin. They had no children.

In 1532 Richard 12th Baron conceived the idea of building a castle close to the border between Meath and Breifne, largely to impress the government with his loyalty. In this project he was supported by his son Christopher but the latter died unexpectedly at the age of 36 leaving five children of whom the eldest, Richard, ultimately became 13th Baron.

The building of Ross Castle began early in 1533. The site chosen was on a high promontory jutting out into the southern end of Loch Sheelin giving a marvellous view over the lake to the north and west. In fact the castle was built on the site of an earlier O'Reilly castle from which John O'Reilly, son of the Felim O'Reilly who died of the plague in 1447, was evicted by the English. The main part of the castle was completed in 1537 and in the following year Richard 12th Baron died.

In 1540 Richard 14th Baron and grandson of Richard the 12th Baron, married Lady Nangle widow of the Baron of Navan. Richard who was 24 years old when he succeeded was subject to frequent depressive attacks, and this combined with his habit of wearing black clothing, caused him to be known as "The Black Baron." He had four children, Sabena born in 1541, Brigid in 1543, Christopher in 1545, and William in 1550.

According to the *Genealogical History of the O'Reillys,*

Ross Castle, on Loch Sheelin built in 1537 by Richard the 12th Baron of Delvin. Today it is the modern residence of a member of the Nugent family.

Edmond of Kilnacrott married, as his second wife, in 1564, Lady Elizabeth, the younger daughter of the Black Baron. As far as is known the Black Baron had no daughter called Elizabeth and Mrs. Ahern Getty authoress of the romantic novel *Orwen and Sabina*,[1] says that her name was Brigid, and this would fit in with the *Nugent Pedigree*. Again the *Genealogical History* states that Hugh Conallach married as his second wife, Mary Nugent, daughter of Thomas, son of the Baron of Delvin, but the only Thomas mentioned in the *Nugent Pedigree* was the son of William, youngest son of the Black Baron.

164

From the year 1390 there had been another O'Reilly stronghold on Loch Sheelin, Crover Castle, close to the northeastern shore. There is a strong local legend of a disastrous drowning which involved both families, yet strange to relate, having regard to its dramatic nature, there is no reference to it in any contemporary record, nor in the *O'Reilly Pedigree*, nor in the *Annals of the Four Masters*. This is all the more remarkable when we recall that an earlier incident when several members of the Crover family were lost when crossing the lake in 1418, was fully documented in the *Annals of Ulster*, the *Annals of Loch Ce*, and the *Four Masters*.

In 1558 Sabina, eldest daughter of the Black Baron, then aged 18, was walking along the bank of the River Inny which formed the boundary of the Breifne territory, when a young stranger stepped ashore from a boat and introduced himself as Orwen, son of the Chief of Clanmahon. This was the first of many meetings which led to a deep romantic relationship between Sabina and Eoghan, which was Orwen's proper name. The situation was fraught with danger for everyone because of the embargo placed by the government on marriages between the English and the native families. The couple decided to elope and marry in secret, this with the approval of Sabina's mother who had now become aware of the situation.

A few days before the date set for the elopement, the lovers arranged to go for an evening sail on the lake, accompanied by Lady Sabina's brother, William. It was a beautiful calm evening when they set out but within a short time a terrific storm blew up and the party was driven onto some rocks; the boat was smashed to pieces and all three occupants were thrown into the water. The rocks, known as "Curry's Rocks" were no great distance from the shore but in the prevailing conditions the frantic retainers watching from the shore were powerless to help. Then, as suddenly as it had arisen, the storm abated, and the watchers could then see William struggling towards the shore carrying his sister in his arms; of Eoghan there was no trace. Then one of the watchers, wading through the shallow water, found the body of Eoghan held fast by one of the jagged rocks on which his clothing had been caught.

Sabina never recovered from the shock and she died a few days later. By agreement of both families the lovers were interred together on a little hillock to the south of Ross Castle. Regular visits were paid to the grave by the family and the principal retainers. One of the latter suggested that at each visit a stone should be placed on the site so that by the end of the season a circular cairn would be well started, and by two years it would be ready for the erection of a modest Celtic cross. As a consequence, to this day one can visit the grave and see the stones, which have never been removed; one can also see the broken shaft with the cross in the circle, lying beside it.² The romance and its tragic ending has been commemorated in a poem entitled "The Romance of Orwen and Sabina" by Philip O'Connell³.

In 1559 the Black Baron was killed in a skirmish near Finea and in 1566 his elder son, Christopher, succeeded.

This Christopher was apparently an unscrupulous land grabber. As early as 1567 he had gained a foothold in Breifne by taking up the leases of fourteen rectories belonging to the Abbey of Fore in Westmeath. Towards the end of Elizabeth's reign he held command of troops in the counties of Cavan and Longford and was granted some escheated lands belonging to various O'Reillys. On the death of Edmond of Kilnacrott he practically obtained the lordship of Clanmahon. His own rebellion in 1607 entailed the forfeiture of his lands but most of these were re-granted to his widow and her son, Sir Richard Nugent. As a result of his rebellion he was imprisoned in Dublin Castle from which he escaped. He

The grave of Orwen and Sabina, two young lovers whose affair ended tragically with Orwen's drowning in Loch Sheelin and Sabina
dying a few days later from grief.

was recaptured and taken to England but was eventually
pardoned.[4]

During the next 30 years the Nugents acquired
further estates, some, of the lands of the O'Reillys who
had been attainted. It is not clear whether Sir Richard,
15th Baron, resided in County Cavan, but he was followed into Breifne by his kinsmen Christopher, Edward,
and Edmund, who all received small portions; Chris-

topher received the old family estate of Racraveen which had been built before the Plantation, and which had been originally filched from the O'Reillys; at times he appears to have resided at Bellananagh. In 1621 he was created first Earl of Westmeath. A descendant, John Nugent, 5th Earl of Westmeath (1672-1754) was the last Catholic holder of the title.

In the *Calendar of State Papers* under the date February 5th 1591, as quoted by Mrs Anne Ahern Getty,[5] the following sinister account appears:

Declaration of Shawne Mc Negawne alias Shane Mc Congawny. . . . that he was entertained by William Nugent in his house at Ross and afterwards appointed to be priest at Killighe. A horseload of Aquavitae was carried into Munsterolys by Patrick Brady to Brian O'Rourke. Edmund Reagh O'Reilly made a faithful promise to the said Brian O'Rourke that he would assist him in his rebellion. (Copy certified by the Lord Deputy and Council 1592, Nov. 20th.)

This Shawn McCongawny seems to have been a spy from the Dublin Council who were interested in pinning something on the Tanist of Breifne to implicate him in the rebellion of Sir Brian O'Rourke who was murdered at Tyburn in 1591. Thus had been brought about the attainder of Edmond of Kilnacrott after his death in 1601. Following the attainder most of his lands were granted to the Nugents.

The Nugents themselves were deprived of their lands under Cromwell's Act of Settlement, passing to one Baines, a clerk. In 1864 a Mrs O'Reilly-Dease of Turbotstown, County Westmeath purchased the Ross estate from the then owners, the Somervilles of Athlumney and carried out extensive repairs and renovations. Unfortunately a few years later a party of picnickers lit a fire on the lead roof which collapsed and the interior, being exposed to the elements rapidly fell into ruins.

Mrs. O'Reilly-Dease had a plate inserted in the castle wall stating that "Myles the Slasher," so called, spent the night before the battle of Finea in Ross Castle, his grandmother's old home said to be Anne Nugent, daughter of Sir William and granddaughter of the "Black Baron." Anna Maria O'Reilly-Dease claimed to be his lineal descendant.

There is no historical warrant whatever for this story. It has been shown that there never was a Myles O'Reilly at the bridge of Finea; his correct pedigree has been given on page 112 supra and that of the true "Myles the Slashed" on page 114.

It is pleasant to be able to add a happy ending to the sad story of Ross Castle. In 1965 it was purchased by another Nugent who has restored it and converted it into a modern residence.

The MacCabes

The MacCabes have always been prominent in Breifne and indeed almost as numerous as the O'Reillys in whose varying fortunes they shared. A well known member of the family was Cathaoir MacCabe, the Cavan bard who died in 1740.

Another distinguished member of the family was Father Felix MacCabe, chaplain to one of the noble families of France. Father MacCabe was born about 1750 at Moyne Hall in the parish of Annegeliffe, a few miles south of Cavan town; the site of "McCabe's castle" may still be seen there. Father MacCabe's grandfather Bernard was the grandson of Alexander MacCabe of Moyne Hall whose lands were declared forfeit after the battle of Aughrim in 1691. Many of Father MacCabe's ancestors figure in the French military records. One of them, Captain Alexander MacCabe, served in the regiment of Chevalier William Wallace for the expedition to Scotland. His brevet was signed by James II on April 21st

1692. James also granted him a coat of arms. The battle axe was prominent in the coats of arms of all branches of the family and good examples may be seen on the MacCabe tomb in Gallon churchyard, Killeshandra, and also on a headstone erected in Kildrumsheridan churchyard near Cootehill by Father Patrick MacCabe, parish priest of Knockbride in 1750, in memory of his parents. The family motto is *Aut vincere aut mori*.[6]

The Bradys

Originally the family name was properly "Mac Brady" but the Mac has long been dropped by most branches of the family; the family has been prominent in Breifne from very early times. The first entry relating to them occurs in the *Annals of the Four Masters* under the year 1256. In common with the O'Reillys and the O'Rourkes the Bradys were descended from Aodh Finn. Their immediate ancestor was Cearbhall, son of Maolmordha who was the ancestor of both the O'Reillys and the Bradys. The territory of the clan was Cuil Brighdin, which comprised the greater part of the parishes of Castletara, Drung, and Larah. Later Cuil Brighdin became co-extensive with Castletara.

One of the early bishops of Kilmore was Nicholas Mac Brady who was the victim of a curious mistake; in 1408 David O'Farrelly rector of the church of Saint Brigid of Disertfynchil (Kildrumsheridan) was visiting Rome and while there it was reported to the papal court that Bishop Mac Brady had died. Whereupon Pope Gregory XII appointed David to the Bishopric of Kilmore and had him consecrated. Of course, on his return home he found that Bishop Mac Brady was very much alive. As a result David O'Farrelly's appointment had to be cancelled. Bishop Mac Brady in fact died in 1421 after an episcopate of twenty-four years. The *Four Masters* described him as a man distinguished for wisdom, piety, chastity, and purity.

In 1444, Andrew Mac Brady, Archdeacon of Kilmore and Rural Dean of Drumlane, was appointed bishop of the diocese. His great achievement was the raising of the ancient church of St. Felimy, Kilmore, to cathedral status, installing in it thirteen canons. He died in 1455.

Another bishop of Kilmore was Thomas Mac Brady who succeeded Bishop John O'Reilly in 1480. He was the son of Andrew Mac Brady of Castletara, where he was born about the year 1444. He died in 1511 at Dromahaire, County Leitrim where he had gone to consecrate the Franciscan Monastery founded by O Ruairc in 1508. He was buried in the Franciscan Monastery of Cavan and his obit in the *Annals of the Four Masters* describes him as a paragon of wisdom and piety, a luminous lamp which enlightened the laity and clergy by instruction and preaching; and a faithful shepherd of the church; after having ordained priests and persons in every degree, after having consecrated many churches and cemeteries, after having bestowed rich presents and food on the poor and the mighty, gave up his spirit to heaven on the 4th of the Calends of March (or August). This extract shows that he died on February 26th, or July 29th, of 1511, aged sixty-seven. He was buried in the monastery of Cavan; he was probably a Franciscan.[7]

Another Mac Brady, John, was bishop of Kilmore from 1540 to 1559. He was the parish priest of Kildrumfertan and by permission of Pope Paul III he was allowed to retain his parochial church. He was a staunch opponent of the so-called Reformation and after a strenous episcopate, he died in 1559.

The next member of the family to occupy the episcopate was Richard Brady. O.F.M. who was appointed in 1580. He lived during the stormy period of Elizabeth I—a persecution in which he suffered great personal distress. He was outstanding in his knowledge of canon and civil law, and was a distinguished jurist. In 1576 he was appointed to the bishopric of Ardagh diocese where he remained until 1580, when Pope Gregory XIII translated him to Kilmore.

In 1585 Queen Elizabeth attempted to deprive him of the bishopric of Kilmore, and actually appointed John Garvey, Protestant Dean of Christchurch Cathedral, in his place. Needless to say the pseudo bishop was unable to take possession of the See and Bishop Brady continued in office. However, in 1590 plans were laid to arrest the bishop; in the *State Papers* of may 1591 it is recorded that the Lord Deputy and others . . . had used all means they could devise for the apprehension of the Popish Bishop of Kilmore. . . .The bishop is most secretly harboured by the Nugents, especially the Baron of Delvin. Bishop Brady, now advanced in years, retired to the Franciscan Abbey of Multyfarnham, near Mullingar, which thenceforth he rarely left, but in 1601 the abbey was raided by the English; Bishop Brady together with a number of friars was arrested and the monastery was set on fire.

The Bishop was first imprisoned in the Castle of Ballymore but later was allowed to reside with a Catholic nobleman living in the neighbourhood on condition that he presented himself to the authorities in Dublin at the close of the winter. He travelled to Dublin towards the end of March 1602 and immediately on arrival was arrested and thrown into prison, where he remained until the summer when his friends obtained his release on payment of a heavy ransom. He returned then to the monastery at Multyfarnham which had been partly rebuilt, but towards the end of the year the monastery was again raided and burnt. The Bishop was again arrested but owing to his decrepitude he was unable to walk so he was beaten up and flung into a brake of briars where he was left for dead. Despite this treatment he survived, to return once more to the monastery where he continued to reside until his death in 1607; he was buried there in the cloisters.

One of the most interesting characters in the family was Fiachra Mac Brady from Stradone in the parish of Laragh. He eked out a precarious livelihood as an itinerant harper visiting fairs and other gatherings in Cavan and the neighbouring counties. He flourished in the early seventeen hundreds and was known as the "Bard of Stradone." He was really a schoolmaster who, to evade the penalties of the law, disguised himself as a harper travelling about the country.

Another Brady, Felim, was the subject of a ballad, "The Bould Felim Brady, the Bard of Armagh," but in fact the original "Bard of Armagh" was Dr. Patrick Donnelly Bishop of Dromore who, in the course of his travels met Fiachra Mac Brady, and being a skilled piper realised how, disguised in piper's garb he would be able to move about freely without fear of arrest; indeed it is recorded that on one occasion, having celebrated Mass on the slopes of Slieve Gallion, afterwards in his guise of a forlorn piper, and thoroughly exhausted, he sat down by the roadside and fell fast asleep. He was discovered by a party of soldiers who roused him, called for music, and danced merrily. They were so pleased with his performance that they made a collection for him and presented him with an overcoat, a welcome Christmas gift.[8]

The *Four Masters* record under the year 1588 an indenture by Myles O'Reilly Chieftain of Breifne and his son Hugh granting one Bernard, son of Donagh, son of David Mac Brady, a merchant of the town of Navan, "the unoccupied area of one street and the stream which runs through Cavan, and which is called Blatach, on condition of building a water mill and building houses along the whole length of the street."[9]

General Thomas Brady (1752-1827) was the son of a Cootehill farmer. Originally he went to Vienna to study for the priesthood but was induced by the Empress Maria Theresa to enter the Austrian Army. He rose rapidly in the ranks and distinguished himself at the storming of Novi, on November 3rd 1788; for his gallantry he was awarded the Cross of the Knights of Maria Theresa. He was promoted to Major General in 1796, Lieutenant General in 1801, and in 1804 was appointed Governor of Dalmatia; in 1807 he was made a Privy Councillor. He married an offshoot of the Austrian Imperial family and died without issue in Vienna on October 14th 1827.

Colonel James Bernard Mac Brady of Loughtee was born in the townland of Dreenan in Kilmore parish in 1732. He went to Austria in 1749, joined the Sincere Infantry Regiment as a volunteer and served as a captain throughout the Seven Years War. The Cross of the Knights of Maria Theresa was conferred on him for gallantry at Schweidnitz in October 1762 and he was created a baron. He was appointed Major to the Hildbringheimer Infantry Regiment in 1768, and a few years later he retired as Colonel. He died in Vienna in 1800.[10]

The Brady Arms

Sable in the sinister base a dexter hand couped at the wrist proper pointing with index finger to the sun in splendour in dexter chief or.

The Cavan Crozier

The crozier of the Mac Bradys is preserved in the Royal Irish Academy collection in the National Museum, Dublin. It belonged to County Cavan, but the exact locality is unknown. The crozier is of bronze and is about 13 inches in length. There is a head or crook, and a short portion of the stem with two knops. It reveals little

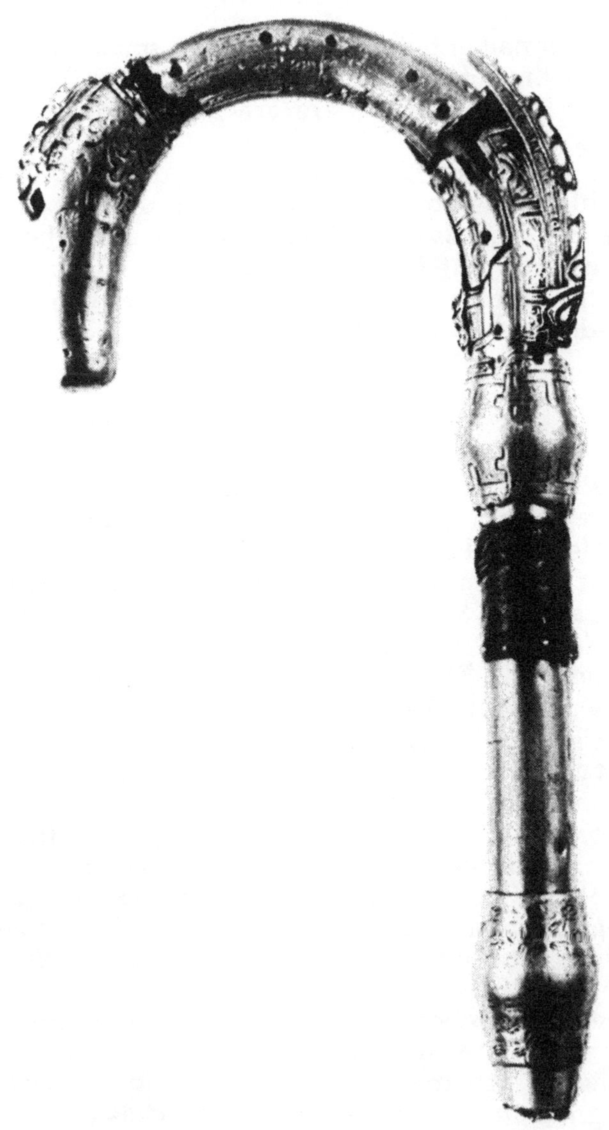

The Cavan Crozier, staff of the early Mac Brady bishops which had to be hidden in order to preserve it during the Reformation.

attempt at ornamentation. A number of small crosses are incised on the uppermost knop. The curved part is divided into panels, and there are some remains of an openwork crest.

It is sometimes called the crozier of the O'Bradys, and its history is obscure. Certain it is that it belonged to some of the early Mac Brady bishops. Like the other Irish croziers, that is those which have survived the fanaticism of the Reformation period, it remained in some hidden place until brighter days dawned.[11]

The Magaurans

The original name was "Mac Samhadhrain" signifying descent through Samhrdran chief of Tullyhaw from Eochy Moyvane High King of Ireland in the fourth century. They had strongholds at Bawnboy, Ballymagauran, and Lissanover. Several of their chiefs were mentioned in the *Annals of the Four Masters* under the years 1485, 1486, and 1512. The genealogy of the family, compiled by O'Clery about 1650 is in his *Book of Genealogies* in the Royal Irish Academy, MS, 23. D 17. The fullest account of the family is given in the "Magauran Dunaire" now in the possession of The Honourable O'Conor Don. It is a mid-fourteenth century vellum containing fifty-four pages of family poems in Irish. It appears to have been compiled by Rory O'Keenan for Thomas Magauran, chief of Tullyhaw who died in 1343. The date of compilation was between the years 1339–1343. O'Keenan himself died in 1387.[12]

Several members of the family were distinguished clerics. Cormac Magauran, a canon of Drumlane, became bishop of Ardagh in 1444 and held the seat until he resigned in 1467 to return to the cloister. Another Magauran, Thady, was bishop of Kilmore from 1455 to 1465. A later Cormac Magauran who was Prior of Drumlane was appointed bishop of Kilmore in 1476 but his appointment was not confirmed; there was some doubt about his legitimacy. In 1480 his appointment was annulled and Thomas Mac Brady was elected. Nevertheless, Cormac continued to press his claims with considerable vigor, causing much trouble to the diocese. He consistently described himself as a bishop of Kilmore until his death in 1512.[13]

The Sheridans

The Sheridans were a family long resident in Breifne and distinguished for their outstanding literary and artistic talent. They came originally from Longford (*vide ante,* page 66) where they were Erenaghs of Granard. The word "erenagh" denotes a steward of church lands. Originally an ecclesiastical office, it later passed into lay hands as an hereditary emolument. In early times the Sheridans were devoted followers of the O'Reilly clan. The name was originally "O'Sirideain" meaning the descendants of Siridean, but the "O" was dropped early in the seventeenth century. One member of the family, Hugh O'Sheridan, was bishop of Kilmore from 1560 to 1579. At the time of his appointment Breifne was in a troubled state owing to the constant endeavors of the native chieftains to drive out the English. The bishop strongly opposed the doctrines of the so-called Reformation and stood firmly against the inroads of heresy. Unfortunately, his health failed and after much suffering he died towards the end of 1579. Other members of the family, however, conformed to the Established Church. Denis Sheridan, who was born in 1612, co-operated with Bishop Bedell in translating the Bible into Irish; his son William Sheridan was Protestant bishop of Kilmore from 1636–1711. The Reverend Thomas Sheridan, D.D. was headmaster of the Royal School, Cavan. He lived at Quilca near Virginia, where he often entertained his lifelong friend, Dean Swift.

Another Thomas Sheridan (1647–1712) was a close follower of James II, while his son Thomas (1684–1746) was tutor in exile to Prince Charles "the Young Pretender," but perhaps the most famous of all was Richard Brinsley Sheridan (1751–1816), author of *The Rivals* and *School for Scandal.* [14]

Finally we must not forget General Philip Henry Sheridan (1831–1888) the renowned and successful commander in the American Civil War. His ancestors belonged to the parish of Killinkere where they had lived for generations. His grandfather, Jack Sheridan, had a farm of nine acres in the townland of Carrickgorman. His son, John, the father of the general, married a Mary Meenagh or Mooney from the same parish. Their two eldest children, Pat and Rose, were born there. Considerable doubt exists as to where their third child, Phil, was born, whether in Killinkere, before the departure of the family to America, or after their arrival there. There is a story that a kindly neighbor, John Smith of Corduagh, took the whole family in his cart to Drogheda on their way to Liverpool. He always insisted that there were three children, one of whom was carried in the mother's arms, and that this was Phil. On the other hand, years later, the mother, then aged eighty-six, maintained that Phil was born in Somerset, Perry County, Ohio, on March 6th 1831. The pros and cons of the argument are fully set out by Rev. Joseph B. Meehan, P.P. M.R.I.A., in *Breifne*, Vol. 11. No. 7 (1964).

And some there be, which have no memorial;
. . . but their glory shall not be blotted out.

—Ecclesiasticus

It is fitting that the story of Breifne should end with an account of one of the last of the O'Reillys to take up arms for his country. "John Kevin O'Reilly, 1916 patriot,

178

General Philip Sheridan, American Civil War commander whose parents moved to America from Beagh, Killinkere, in or around 1831.

is best remembered for his well known marching song
'Wrap the Green Flag Round Me Boys.' Born in Cavan
Town, he moved to Dublin where he met and married a
local girl, Catherine Curran. From his home at 181 North
Circular Road, in Dublin, he involved himself in the
struggle for freedom and in 1916 he and his five sons,
Kevin, Samuel, Desmond, Thomas and Donal fought in
the famous G.P.O. garrison. An auditor with the First
Dail, Mr. O'Reilly died on April 26, 1929, aged 66."[14]

Notes

1. *Orwen & Sabina. An Historical Novel of 16th Century Ireland.*
Vantage Press. Inc. 120 West 31st St. New York By Mrs A. Ahern-
Getty.
2. Op. cit.
3. "A Crosserlough Poet & Essayist." O'Connell. Breifne. 1962.

Notes on the Annals

The Annals of the Four Masters. These were originally compiled by four Franciscan monks during the period 1630–1636. They purport to cover the history of Ireland from "the year of the world" 2242 to A.D. 1616. They were translated from the original Irish and edited by John O'Donovan in four volumes. Published by Hodges and Smith Dublin (1851)

The Annals of Ulster. A chronicle of Irish affairs from A.D. 431–1540. Original author doubtful. They were translated and edited, in four volumes by William M. Hennessy. Published by Alexander Thom and Co. Ltd, Dublin (1887).

The Annals of Loch Cé. These were written by a monk, Brian McDermott, who lived in a monastery on an island in Loch Cé, County Roscommon. They cover the period from A.D.1014–1590. They were translated and edited by William M. Hennessy in 1871.

Copies of all the Annals are in the National Library of Ireland, Kildare Street, Dublin.

The Principal Lines of the O'Reilly Pedigree

Raghallach
(d.1014)

Airten

Airghiallach
Cu-Connacht
(d.1089)

Mac na hOidche
(d.1127)

Godfraidh
(d.1161)

Cathal na gCaorach
(d.1162)

Annadh
(d.1220)

Cathal na Beitighe
(d.1256)

Domhnall Mor   Niall an Caoch
(d.1256)   (d.1256)

Feargall an fochar   Giolla Iosa Ruadh   Matha na nUball
(C.1281-1293)   (C.1293-1330)   (C.1256-1281)

Cu-Connacht   Philip   Domhnall   Mathgamain
(C.1330-1365)   (C.1365-1384)   (d.1400)

                Maolmordha   Sean   Thomas
                (C.1401-1411)   (C.1390-1401)   (C.1384-1390)

Concubar   Eoghan na Feisoge   Felimy   Richard Mor
(d.1436)   (C.1418-1449)   (d.1447)

Thomas Oge   Sean an Einigh   Aodh Orosach   Cathal   Richard Oge
(d.1421)   (C.1449-1460)   (d.1460)   (C.1460-1468)   (C.1411-1418)
                Turlough
                (C.1468-1487)

                Sean   Cathal
            (C.1487-1491)   (d.1497)

Sean   Aodh   Eoghan Ruadh   Philip
(C.1491-1510)   (C.1510-1514)   (C.1514-1526)   (d.1514)

Feargal   Maolmordha   Turlough   Cahir
(C.1526-1535)   (C.1535-1565)   (d.1495)   (d.1538)

Aodh

Brian an   Maolmordha
Chogaidh
(d.s.p.)   Hugh the Primate
                     (1581-1653)

Aodh Conallach   Cahir   Edmond of Kilnacrott   Philip the Prior
(C.1565-1585)   (C.1596-1601)
                                                          Maelmore
                                                          John of Dromore
                                                          Terence
                                                          Farrell the Bishop
                                                          (1741-1829)

C.= Chief of Breifne

d.= died

d.s.p.= died without issue

The Line of Aodh Conallach
(Sir Hugh O'Reilly)
Daughter of Betagh 1 = = 2 Mary Nugent
of Moynalty
Sean Ruadh
(Sir John)
(C.1583-1596)
Philip
(C.1596)
Eoghan
(C.1601-1609)
Maolmordha
Lucas
Maolmordha
Breagh
(C.1596-1598)
Maolmordha Oge
Captain Hugh
(d.1628)
Philip
Sean
the Friar
Shane
Mulmore
Aodh
(d.1598)
Maolmordha
(d.1653)
Sean
(d.1634)
Hugh Boy
Turlough
Edmund of
Dunmurry
Hugh of
Manhill
Mulmorey Mc Hugh
Mc Shane
Philip Mc Hugh
Mc Shane
Emonn Buidhe
(d.1693)
Luke
Hugh
(d.1711)
Aodh Ruadh
Eibhlin
Eoghan
(d.1753)
"Colonel" Myles
Aodh Oge
(drowned 1617)
Philip
Edmond
Edmond
Emonn
Philip
Maolmordha
"The Renowned Colonel"
(d.1670)
Maolmordha Oge
Philip
Emonn

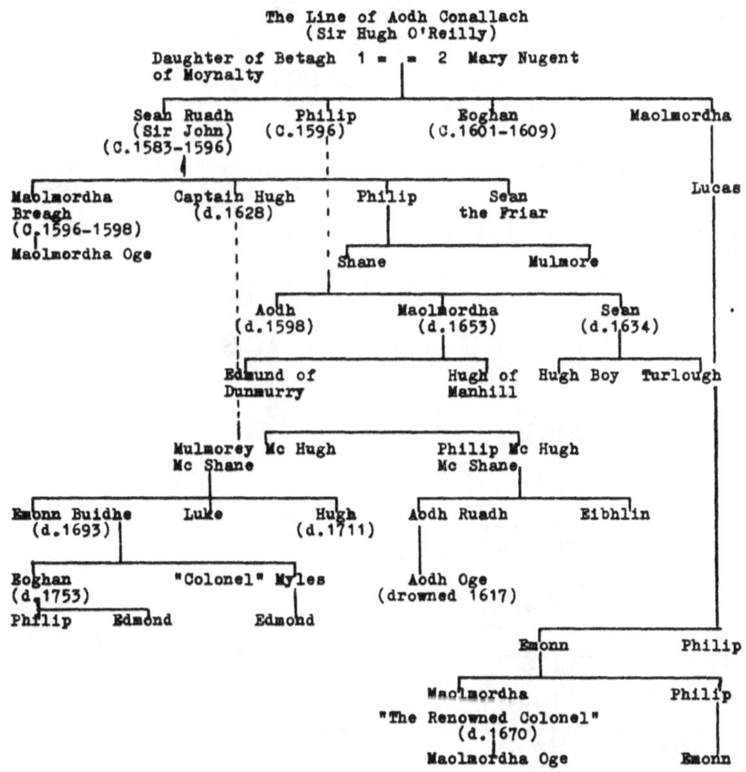

183

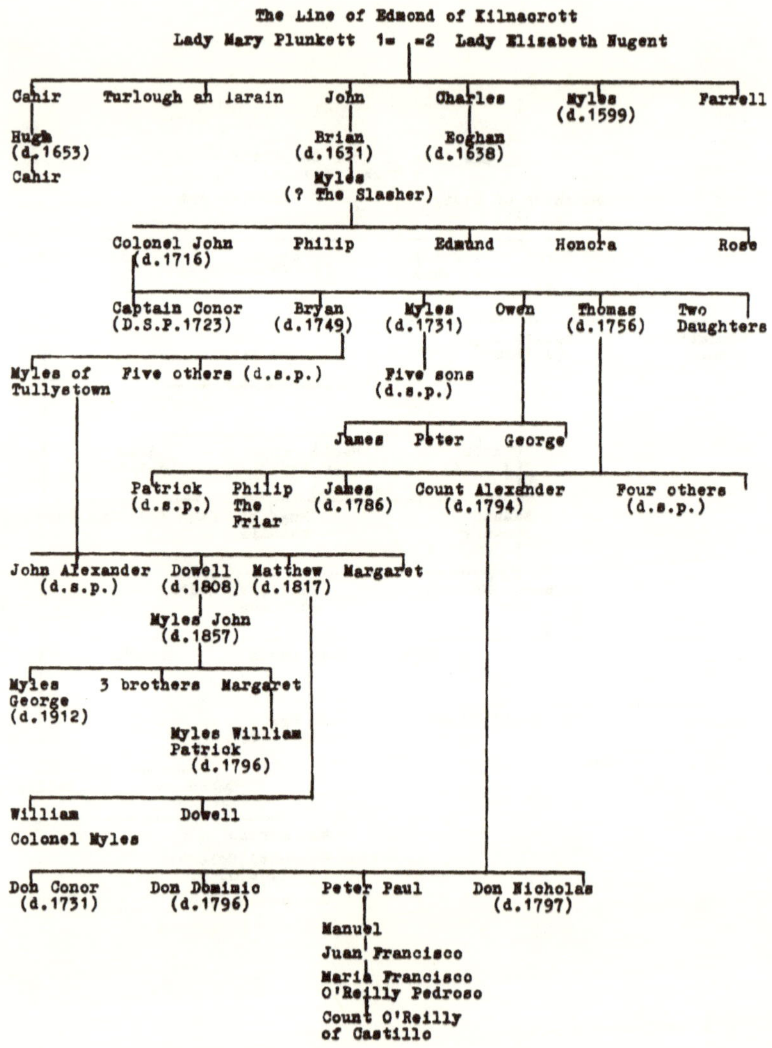

The Line of Edmond of Kilnacrott
Lady Mary Plunkett 1= =2 Lady Elizabeth Nugent
Cahir   Turlough an larain   John   Charles   Myles (d.1599)   Farrell
Hugh (d.1653)
Cahir
Brian (d.1631)
Eoghan (d.1638)
Myles (? The Slasher)
Colonel John (d.1716)   Philip   Edmund   Honora   Rose
Captain Conor (D.S.P.1723)   Bryan (d.1749)   Myles (d.1731)   Owen   Thomas (d.1756)   Two Daughters
Myles of Tullystown   Five others (d.s.p.)   Five sons (d.s.p.)
James   Peter   George
Patrick (d.s.p.)   Philip The Friar   James (d.1786)   Count Alexander (d.1794)   Four others (d.s.p.)
John Alexander (d.s.p.)   Dowell (d.1808)   Matthew (d.1817)   Margaret
Myles John (d.1857)
Myles George (d.1912)   3 brothers   Margaret
Myles William Patrick (d.1796)
William   Dowell
Colonel Myles
Don Conor (d.1731)   Don Dominic (d.1796)   Peter Paul   Don Nicholas (d.1797)
Manuel
Juan Francisco
Maria Francisco O'Reilly Pedroso
Count O'Reilly of Castillo

Some of the other titles in the Irish History Classic series
published by The Long Riders' Guild Press.
We are constantly adding to our collection, so for an
up-to-date list please visit our website:
www.thelongridersguild.com

The History of Breifne O'Reilly	J. J. O'Reilly
Poems on the O'Reillys	James Carney
Genealogical History of the O'Reillys	James Carney
Irish Pedigree – the Origin of the Irish Nation – Volume One	John O'Hart
Irish Pedigree – the Origin of the Irish Nation – Volume Two	John O'Hart
Irish Pedigree – the Origin of the Irish Nation – Volume Three	John O'Hart
Irish Pedigree – the Origin of the Irish Nation – Volume Four	John O'Hart

The Long Riders' Guild
The world's leading source of information regarding equestrian exploration!
www.thelongridersguild.com